Differentiating Instruction With Menus

U.S. History

ADVANCED-LEVEL MENUS
Grades 9–12

Differentiating Instruction With Menus

U.S. History

Laurie E. Westphal, Ed.D.

PRUFROCK PRESS INC.
WACO, TEXAS

Copyright ©2020, Prufrock Press Inc.

Edited by Katy McDowall

Cover and layout design by Allegra Denbo

ISBN-13: 978-1-64632-054-7

Printed in the United States of America.

At the time of this book's publication, all facts and figures cited are the most current available; all telephone numbers, addresses, and website URLs are accurate and active; all publications, organizations, websites, and other resources exist as described in this book; and all have been verified. The author and Prufrock Press make no warranty or guarantee concerning the information and materials given out by organizations or content found at websites, and we are not responsible for any changes that occur after this book's publication. If you find an error or believe that a resource listed here is not as described, please contact Prufrock Press.

Prufrock Press Inc.
P.O. Box 8813
Waco, TX 76714-8813
Phone: (800) 998-2208
Fax: (800) 240-0333
http://www.prufrock.com

CONTENTS

Chapter 9: The Cold War Through Present Day **133**

PART I

All About Menus and Choice

CHAPTER 1

Choice

"For so many reasons, it is simply the right thing to do for this age group."

—Shared by a group of secondary teachers when asked why choice is important for their students

Why Is Choice Important?

Ask any adult if they would prefer to choose what to do or be told what to do, and of course, they are going to prefer the choice. Students, especially teenagers, have these same feelings. Although they may not always stand up and demand a choice if none are present, they benefit in many ways from having them.

One benefit of choice is its ability to meet the needs of so many different students and their varied learning preferences. The Dunedin College of Education (Keen, 2001) conducted a research study on the preferred learning styles of 250 gifted students. Students were asked to rank different learning options. Of the 13 different options described to the students, only one option did not receive at least one negative response, and that was choice. Although all students have different preferences, choice is the one option that meets all students' needs. Why? Well, it takes the focus from the teacher as the decision maker and allows students to decide what is best for them. What teenager would argue against being able to do something that they prefer to do? When given the opportunity to choose, students are going to choose what best fits their educational needs.

"I really was not sure how my students were going to react to these choices. I didn't want the menu to be viewed as busy work when we already had so much content to cover. I was surprised (and relieved) by how well they responded [to the choices]. Now, they want to have choice in everything, which is always up for negotiation."

—English II teacher

Another benefit of choice is its ability to address different learning preferences and ultimately offer the opportunity to better assess what students understand about the content being studied. During professional development, I often ask teachers what learning preferences are most addressed in the products they provide. Not surprisingly, visual and written products top the list. These two preferences are most popular for many reasons, including ease of grading, ease of organizing and managing, and lack of supplies needed. In looking back on all of the different products my students have created, however, I noticed that most often, the tactile, kinesthetic, and verbal products provided greater depth and complexity (Komarraju et al., 2011). After analyzing these "noisy" products, I have come to realize that if I really want to know what my students understand, I need to allow them to show me through their learning preference—and the most common preferences of my students are not visual-written. Most students prefer tactile-kinesthetic (Dunn & Honigsfeld, 2013; Ricca, 1984; Sagan, 2010; Snyder, 1999). Because these preferences are not always addressed during whole-class instruction, teachers need a strategy that can allow students to express themselves. Using choice to offer these opportunities can help address the needs of more students in our classrooms.

Another advantage of choice is a greater sense of independence for the students (Deci et al., 1991; Patall, 2013; Robinson et al., 2008). When teachers offer choice, students design and create a product based on what they envision, rather than what their teacher envisions. When students would enter my classroom, many times they had been trained by previous teachers to produce what the teacher wanted, not what the students thought would be best. Teaching my students that what they envision could be correct (and wonderful) could be a struggle. "Is this what you want?" or "Is this right?" were popular questions as we started the school year. As we progressed, and I continued to redirect their questions back to them ("Is that what you would like to show?" or "Does that seem right to you?"), students began to ask for my approval less; they became more independent in their work. They might still need assurance, but the phrasing was different, "This is what I have so far. Can I ask for help from Joe?" or "I don't like this; I am going to pick something else." When teachers allow students choice in the products they create to show their learning, the students can develop this independence.

Increased student focus and persistence is another benefit of offering choice. When students are making choices in the activities they wish to complete, they are more focused on the learning that is needed to create their choice products (Flowerday & Schraw, 2003; Ricca, 1984). Students become engaged when they learn information that can help them develop products that they are excited about creating. Many students struggle with the purpose of the information being taught in the classroom, and this can lead to behavior problems. Students may feel disconnected from the content and lose interest (Robinson et al., 2008). Instead, students will pay closer attention to instruction when an immediate application (the student's choice product) for the knowledge being presented in class is present. If students are excited about the product, they are more focused on the content; they are less likely to be off task during instruction.

Many a great educator has referred to the idea that the best learning takes place when the students have a desire to learn. Some students have a desire to learn anything that is new to them; others do not want to learn anything unless it has interest for them. By incorporating choice activities that require the students to stretch beyond what they already know, teachers create a void which needs to be filled. This void leads to a desire to learn.

A Point to Ponder: Making Good Choices Is a Skill

"I want my students to be independent, and it can be frustrating that they just can't make decisions for themselves. I hadn't thought I might need to actually teach decision-making skills."

—Secondary study skills teacher, after hearing me discuss choice as a skill

When we think of making a good choice as a skill, much like writing an effective paragraph or essay, it becomes easy enough to understand that we need to encourage students to make their own choices. In keeping with this analogy, students could certainly figure out how to write on their own, and perhaps even how to compose sentences and paragraphs, by modeling other examples. Imagine, however, the progress and strength of the writing produced when students are given guidance and even the most basic of instruction on how to accomplish the task. The written piece is still their own, but the quality of the finished piece is much stronger when guidance is given during the process. There is a reason why class time is spent in the AP classroom focusing on how to write an appropriate response to a document-based question (DBQ) or free-response question (FRQ). Students need to practice the skill before the big test in May. The same is true with choices; the quality of choices our high school students can make in the classroom is directly impacted by exposure and practice.

As with writing, students could make choices on their own, but when the teacher provides background knowledge and assistance, the choices become more meaningful and the products richer. All students certainly need guidance (even if our strong-willed high school students think they know it all), as the idea of choice may be new to them. Some students may only have experienced basic instructional choices, like choosing between two journal prompts or perhaps having the option of making either a poster or a PowerPoint presentation about the content being studied. Some may not have experienced even this level of choice. This lack of experience can cause frustration for both teacher and student.

Teaching Choices as a Skill

So, what is the best way to provide guidance and enable our students to develop the skill of making good choices while still allowing them to develop their individuality? First, choose the appropriate number of choices for your students. Although the goal might be to have students choose from 20 different options, teachers might start by having their students choose from three predetermined choices the first day (if they were using a game show menu, for instance, students might choose an activity from the first column). Then, after that product had been created, students could choose from another three options from another column a few days later, and perhaps from another three the following week. By breaking students' choices down, teachers reinforce how to approach or attack a more complex and/or varied choice format in the future. All students can work up to making complex choices from longer lists of options as their choice skill level increases.

Second, although our high school students feel they know everything now, they may still need guidance on how to select the option that is right for them. They may not automatically gravitate toward options without an exciting and detailed description of each choice. For the most part, students have been trained to produce what the teacher requests, which means that when given a choice, they may choose what seems to be the easiest and what the teacher most wants (then they can get to what they would prefer to be doing). This means that when the teacher discusses the different menu options, they must be equally as excited about each option. The discussion of the different choices must be somewhat animated and specific. For example, if the content is all very similar, the focus should be on the product: "If you want to create something you might see on YouTube, this one is for you!" or "If you want to be artistic, check this one as a maybe!" The more exposure students have to the processing the teacher provides, the more skillful they become in their choice making.

How Can Teachers Allow Choice?

"The GT students seem to get more involved in assignments when they have choice. They have so many creative ideas and the menus give them the opportunity to use them."

—Secondary social studies teacher, when asked about how students respond to having choices

When people visit a restaurant, they are all attending with the common goal of finding something on the menu to satisfy their hunger. We all hope that when students come into our classroom, they will have a hunger as well—a hunger for learning. Choice menus are a way of allowing students to choose how they would like to satisfy that hunger. At the very least, a menu is a list of choices that students use to choose an activity (or activities) they would like to complete to show their learning. At best, it is a complex system in which students are given point goals and complete different products to earn points (which are based on the levels of Bloom's revised taxonomy; Anderson & Krathwohl, 2001). These menus should have a way to incorporate a "free choice" option for those picky eaters who would like to make a special order to satisfy their learning hunger.

The next few sections provide examples of different menu formats that will be used in this book. Each menu has benefits, limitations or drawbacks, and time considerations. An explanation of the free choice option and its management will follow the information on each type of menu.

Tic-Tac-Toe Menu

"My students really enjoy the Tic-Tac-Toe menus, and I get them to stretch themselves without them realizing it."

– High school AP World Geography teacher

Description

The Tic-Tac-Toe menu (see Figure 1.1) is a well-known, commonly used menu that contains a total of eight predetermined choices and one free choice for students. These choices can range from task statements leading to product creation, complex and/or higher level processing questions, or leveled problems for solving. The choices can be created at the same level of Bloom's revised taxonomy or can be arranged in such a way to allow for the three different levels or objectives within a unit or topic. If all choices have been created at the same level of Bloom's revised taxonomy, then each choice carries the same weight for grading and has similar expectations for completion time and effort.

Benefits

Flexibility. This menu can cover either one topic in depth, three different topics, or three objectives within one content area. When this menu covers just one objective, and all tasks are from the same level of Bloom's revised taxonomy (preferably the highest), students have the option of completing three projects in a tic-tac-toe pattern, or simply picking three from the menu. When the menu covers three objectives, three different levels of Bloom's revised taxonomy, or three different learning preferences, students will need to complete a vertical or horizontal tic-tac-toe pattern only (either a vertical column or horizontal row) to be sure they have completed one activity from each objective, level, and learning style.

Figure 1.1. Tic-Tac-Toe menu example.

Stretching. When students make choices on this menu by completing a row or column based on its design, they will usually face one choice that is out of their comfort zone. This "stretch" may result from a task's level of Bloom's revised taxonomy, its product style, or its content. Students will complete this "uncomfortable" choice because they want to do the other two in that row or column.

Friendly design. Students quickly understand how to use this menu. It is nonthreatening because it does not contain points, and therefore it seems to encourage students to stretch out of their comfort zones.

Weighting. All products are equally weighted, so recording grades and maintaining paperwork are easily accomplished.

Short time period. They are intended for shorter periods of time, between 1–3 weeks based on the tasks found on the menu as well as the amount of class time allotted for students to work on the menu.

Limitations

Few topics. These menus only cover one or three topics.

Student compromise. Although this menu does allow choice, when following the guidelines of rows or columns only, the menu provides only six different ways to meet the goal. This restriction means a student will sometimes have to compromise and complete an activity they would not have chosen because it completes their tic-tac-toe. (This is not always bad, though!)

No "safety net." Because each product in this menu is recorded as its own grade, it is possible that a student could fail this menu. Other formats allow students to make a poor choice and still earn full credit by completing additional options.

Time Considerations

Tic-Tac-Toe menus usually are intended for shorter amounts of completion time—at the most, they could take up to 3 weeks with students working outside of class and submitting one product each week. If a menu focuses on one topic in-depth and the students have time in class to work on their products, the menu could be completed in one week.

Meal Menu

"Seemed pretty easy at first—after all it was only three things and I was thinking I would just have to draw a few equations. All the lunch and dinner real world stuff was hard— [I] had to really think."

—High school Algebra II student

Description

The Meal menu (see Figure 1.2) is a menu with a total of at least nine predetermined choices as well as two or more enrichment/optional activities for students. The choices are created at the various levels of Bloom's revised taxonomy and incorporate different learning preferences, with the levels getting progressively higher and more complex as students progress from breakfast to lunch and then dinner. All products carry the same weight for grading and have similar expectations for completion time and effort. The enrichment or optional (dessert) options can be used for extra credit or replace another meal option at the teacher's discretion.

Benefits

Great starter menu. This menu is very straightforward and easy to understand, so time is saved in presenting the completion expectations.

Flexibility. This menu can cover either one topic in depth or three different objectives or aspects within a topic, with each meal representing a different aspect. With this menu, students have the option of completing three products: one from each meal.

Optional enrichment. Although not required, the dessert category of the Meal menu allows students to have the option of going further or deeper if time during the unit permits. This option could also be used, at teacher discretion, as a replacement of low score on one of the meal products.

Chunkability. The Meal menu is very easy to break apart into smaller pieces. Whether you have students who need support in making choices or you only want to focus on one aspect of a topic at a time, this menu can accommodate these decisions. Students could be asked to select a breakfast while the rest of the menu is put on hold until the breakfast product is submitted, then a lunch product is selected, and so on.

Friendly design. Students quickly understand how to use this menu because of its real-world application.

Weighting. All products are equally weighted, so recording grades and maintaining paperwork are easily accomplished with this menu.

Short time period. Meal menus are intended for shorter periods of time, between 1–3 weeks.

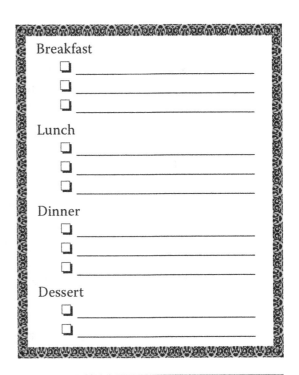

Figure 1.2. Meal menu example.

Limitations

No "safety net." Because each product in this menu is recorded as its own grade, it is possible that a student could fail this menu, unless the teacher allows the optional dessert to replace a low grade on one of the meal products.

Time Considerations

Meal menus usually are intended for shorter amounts of completion time—at the most, they should take 3 weeks with students working outside of class and submitting one product each week. If the menu focuses on one topic in-depth and the students have time in class to work on their products, the menu could be completed in one week.

List Menu/"Challenge List"

"Of the different formats I tried this year, I really liked the challenge list format. I could modify the menu simply by changing the [point] goal. When I had a student test out of two days, I simply upped [their] goal to 140, and [they] worked on [their] menu during instructional time. It was a huge success!"

—Secondary math teacher

Description

The basic List menu (see Figure 1.3), or Challenge List, has a total of at least 10 predetermined choices, each with its own point value, and at least one free choice for students. Choices are simply listed with assigned points based on the levels of Bloom's revised taxonomy. The choices carry different weights and have different expectations for completion time and effort. A point criterion is set forth that equals 100%, and students choose how they wish to attain that point goal. There are different versions of the list menu included in this book: the Challenge List (one topic in depth) and a Multitopic List Menu (which, based on its structure, can accommodate more than one topic).

Benefits

Grade-as-you-go. This menu requires that teachers grade products as the students complete them. Actively grading and providing immediate feedback are important so the students can alter their plans and choose to submit additional products to be sure they reach the point goal. Additionally, by grading-as-you-go, teachers will not have piles of products to grade once the menu is completed.

Responsibility. Students have complete control over their grades. Students like the idea that they can guarantee their grade if they complete their required work and meet the expecta-

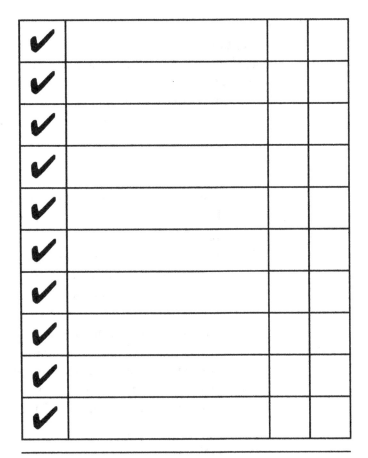

Figure 1.3. List menu example.

tions outlined in the rubric and product guidelines. If students do not earn full credit on one of the chosen products, they can complete another product to be sure they have met their point goal. This responsibility over their own grades also allows a shift in thinking about grades—whereas many students think of grades in terms of how the teacher judged their work, or what the teacher "gave me," having control over their grades leads students to understand that they earn their grades.

Different learning levels. This menu has the flexibility to allow for individualized contracts for different learning levels within the classroom. Because classrooms may have many ability levels, it might be necessary to contract students based on their ability or results from the pretesting of content. In which case, each student can contract for a certain number of points for their 100%.

Concept reinforcement. This menu allows for an in-depth study of the material. With the different levels of Bloom's revised taxonomy being represented, however, students who are at the early stages of learning the concepts can choose lower-level point value products to reinforce the basics before jumping into the higher level activities.

Variety. A list menu offers a larger variety of product choices. There is guaranteed to be a product of interest to everyone. (And if there isn't, there is always free choice!)

Limitations

One topic. If using the traditional challenge list format, this menu can only be used for one topic in depth, so that students cannot miss any specific content.

Cannot guarantee objectives. If the traditional challenge menu is used for more than one topic, it is possible for a student to not have to complete an activity for each objective, depending on the choices they make.

Preparation. Teachers need to have all materials ready at the beginning of the unit for students to be able to choose any of the activities on the list. This expectation requires a degree of advanced planning. (*Note*: This advanced preparation leads to low stress during the unit as all of the materials have already been gathered.)

Time Considerations

List menus usually are intended for shorter amounts of completion time—at the most, 2 weeks. (*Note*: Once you have assembled the materials, the preparation is minimal!)

20-50-80 Menus

"As you suggested, I used one of your 20-50-80 menus as homework to review equations of a line the week before we went into solving systems of equations. It was very easy for the students to understand and saved so much time at the beginning of the systems unit. I am going to use these more often."

—Algebra I teacher

Description

A 20-50-80 menu (see Figure 1.4; Magner, 2000), is a variation on a List menu, with a total of at least eight predetermined choices: no more than two choices with a point value of 20, at least four choices with a point value of 50, and at least two choices with a point value of 80. Choices are assigned these points based on the levels of Bloom's revised taxonomy. Choices with a point value of 20 represent the remember and understand levels, choices with a point value of 50 represent the apply and analyze levels, and choices with a point value of 80 represent the evaluate and create levels. All levels of choices carry different weights and have different expectations for completion time and effort. Students are expected to earn 100 points for a 100%. Students choose what combination of products they would like to complete to attain that point goal.

20 Points
- ☐ _____
- ☐ _____

50 Points
- ☐ _____
- ☐ _____
- ☐ _____
- ☐ _____

80 Points
- ☐ _____
- ☐ _____

Figure 1.4. 20-50-80 menu example.

Benefits

Responsibility. With this menu, students have complete control over goals and their grade. (*Note*: This is not to say that it is acceptable for students to choose 70% as their goal. The expectation is always that the students will work to achieve or exceed the point goal for the menu.)

Guaranteed activity. This menu's design is set up in such a way that students must complete at least one activity at a higher level of Bloom's revised taxonomy to reach their point goal.

Grade-as-you-go. This menu requires that teachers grade products as the students complete them. Actively grading and providing immediate feedback are important so the students can alter their plans and choose to submit additional products to be sure they reach the point goal. Additionally, by grading-as-you-go, teachers will not have piles of products to grade once the menu is completed.

Low stress. This menu is one of the shortest menus. If students choose well and complete quality products, they could accomplish their goal by completing just two products. This menu is usually not as daunting as some of the longer, more complex menus. The 20-50-80 menu provides students a great introduction into the process of making choices.

Limitations

One topic. If this menu is used for more than one topic, it is possible for a student to not have to complete an activity for each objective, depending on the choices they make. Therefore, a 20-50-80 menu is limited in the number of topics it can assess.

Limited higher level thinking. Students could potentially complete only one activity at a higher level of thinking (although many students will complete more to allow themselves a "cushion" in case they do not earn full credit on a product).

Time Considerations

These menus are usually intended for a shorter amount of completion time—at the most, 2 weeks with students working outside of class, or one week, if class time is allowed for product completion.

Game Show Menu

"It was different, doing a [game show] menu. I had to really consider how I was going to get enough points but still do all the topics. By the time I was done, at least I know I got a 100% on a major grade."

—High school U.S. history student

Description

The Game Show menu (see Figure 1.5) is a complex menu. It can cover multiple topics or objectives with three predetermined choices and a free student choice for each objective. Choices are assigned points based on the levels of Bloom's revised taxonomy. All choices carry different weights and have different expectations for completion time and effort. A point criterion is set forth that equals 100%. Students must complete at least one activity from each objective to reach their goal.

Benefits

Free choice. This menu allows the most free choice options of any of the menu formats. Although it has many choices for students, if they do not want to complete the offered activities, students can propose their activity for each objective addressed on the menu.

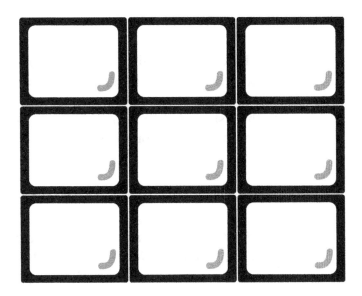

Figure 1.5. Game Show menu example.

Responsibility. This menu allows students to guarantee their grade as long as they meet the point goal for 100%.

Grade-as-you-go. This menu requires that teachers grade products as the students complete them. By grading-as-you-go, teachers will not have piles of products to grade once the menu is completed.

Different learning levels. The game show menu has the flexibility to allow for individualized contracts for different learning levels within the classroom. Each student can create a contract for a certain number of points for their 100%.

Objectives guaranteed. The teacher is guaranteed that the students complete an activity from each objective covered, even if it is at a lower level.

Limitations

Confirm expectations. The only real limitation of the Game Show menu is that students (and parents) must understand the guidelines for completing the menu. Teachers need to remember to copy the instruction page on the back of the menu!

Time Considerations

These menus usually are intended to be completed in a longer amount of time. Although teachers could use these menus yearlong (each column could be a grading period), they usually are intended for 2–3 weeks based on the tasks found on the menu as well as the amount of class time allotted for students to work on the menu.

Free Choice

"History is much more than just dates and events, but sometimes it is difficult for the students to see that. When they get to make history their own is when they begin to move past memorization."

—High school AP History teacher

As a menu option, students may be offered the opportunity to submit a free choice for their teacher's consideration. Figure 1.6 shows two sample proposal forms that have been used many times successfully in my classroom. The form provided to students is based on the type of menu being presented. If using a target-based menu like the Tic-Tac-Toe or Meal menu, there is no need to submit a free-choice proposal form that includes the mention of points.

When implementing a menu that includes free choice, a copy of the appropriate free-choice proposal form should be given to each student when the menu is first introduced. The form should be discussed with the students, so they understand the expectations of proposing a free choice. If they do not want to make a proposal after you have discussed the menu and its activities, the students can place unused forms in a designated place. I always had a box of blank proposal forms on the supply table in my classroom, so unused forms could be returned there. Some students may want to keep their free-choice proposal form "just in case"—you may be surprised who wants to submit a proposal form after hearing about the opportunity!

These proposal forms must be submitted before students begin working on their free choice. That way, the teacher knows what the students are working on, and the student knows the expectations for the product of choice. Once approved, the forms can be stapled to the student's menu sheet for reference. The students can refer to it as they develop their free

Free-Choice Proposal Form for Point-Based Menu

Points Requested:		Points Approved:	

Proposal Outline

1. What specific topic or idea will you learn about?

2. What criteria should be used to grade it? (Neatness, content, creativity, artistic value, etc.)

3. What will your product look like?

4. What materials will you need from the teacher to create this product?

Free-Choice Proposal Form for Menus

Proposal Outline

1. What specific topic or idea will you learn about?

2. What criteria should be used to grade it? (Neatness, content, creativity, artistic value, etc.)

3. What will your product look like?

4. What materials will you need from the teacher to create this product?

Figure 1.6. Free-choice proposal forms.

choice, and when the grading takes place, the teacher can refer to the agreement for the "graded" features of the product.

Each part of the proposal form is important and needs to be discussed with students during the introductory discussion of the form.

- *Name/Teacher's approval.* It is very important that the student submits this form to the teacher. The teacher will carefully review all of the information, give it back to the student for clarification if needed, and then sign the top. Although not always possible, I preferred that the students discuss their forms with me, so we can both be clear about their ideas.

- *Points requested.* Only on the point-based menu proposal form, this is usually where negotiation takes place. Students will often submit their first free-choice request for a very high number of points (even the 100% goal). Students tend to equate the amount of time an activity or product will take with the amount of points it should earn. Unfortunately, the points are always based on the level of Bloom's taxonomy. A PowerPoint with a vocabulary word quiz would get minimal points although it may have taken a long time to create. If the students have not been exposed to the levels of Bloom's taxonomy, the assigning of points can be difficult to explain. Teachers can always refer to the popular "Bloom's Verbs" to help explain the difference between time and higher level activities.

- *Points approved.* Only on the point-based menu proposal form, this is the final decision recorded by the teacher once the point haggling is finished.

- *Proposal outline.* This is where the students will tell you everything about the product that they intend to complete. These questions should be completed in such a way that you can picture what they are planning on completing. These questions also show you that the students know what they are planning on completing as well.
  - *What specific topic or idea will you learn about?* Students need to be specific here, not just "science" or "writing." This response is where the students need look at the objectives or standards of the unit and choose which objective they would like to address through their product.
  - *What criteria should be used to grade it?* Although there are guidelines for all of the projects that the students might create, it is important for the students to explain what criteria

are most important in its evaluation. The student may indicate that the product guideline being used for all of the predetermined product is fine; however, they may also want to add other criteria here.

- *What will your product look like?* It is important that this response be as detailed as possible. If students cannot express what it will "look like," then they have probably not given their free choice enough thought.

- *What materials will you need from the teacher to create this product?* This question is an important consideration. Sometimes students do not have the means to purchase items for their project. These materials can be negotiated as well, but if you ask what students may need, they often will develop even grander ideas for their free choice. This may also be a place for students to note any special equipment or technology needs they may have to create their product.

Chapter 2

How to Use Menus in the Classroom

Instructional menus can be used in different ways in the secondary classroom. To decide how to implement your choice menu, the following questions should be considered:

- How confident are your students in making choices and working independently?
- How much intellectually appropriate information is readily available for students to obtain on their own?
- How much prior knowledge of the topic being taught do the students have before the unit or lesson begins?

After considering the responses to these questions, there is a variety of ways to use menus.

Building Background Knowledge or Accessing Prior Knowledge

"I have students with so many different experiences—sometimes I spend a lot more time than I allotted to review and get everyone up to speed before we get started."

—Secondary social studies teacher

There are many ways to use menus in the classroom. One way that is often overlooked is using menus to review or build background knowledge or access prior knowledge before a unit begins. Using menus this way is beneficial when students have had exposure to upcoming content in the past, perhaps during the previous year's instruction or through life experiences. Many high school students have had preliminary exposure to the basic information needed in their classes. However, students may not remember the details of the content at the depth needed to proceed with the upcoming unit immediately. A shorter menu covering the background or previous year's objectives can be provided the week prior to the new unit. This way, students have the opportunity to recall and engage with the information in a meaningful way, while not using valuable class time during the first day of a new unit to do so. Because the teacher knows that the students have covered the content in the past, the students should be able to work independently on the menu by engaging their prior knowledge. Students work on products from the selected menu as anchor activities and/or homework throughout the week preceding the new unit, with all products being submitted prior to the upcoming unit's initiation. By using menus in this manner, students have been thinking about the upcoming unit for a week and are ready to investigate the topic further. Students are prepared to take their knowledge to a deeper level on the first day of instruction, conserving that much-needed instruction time.

Enrichment and Supplemental Activities

"Just because my students are teenagers doesn't mean they do not need enrichment; the problem is finding time. My curriculum is so packed, and I had always had trouble getting any in. I tried using an enrichment menu for the body systems since I thought we might have enough time. The students really enjoyed it; they seemed to make time for it. I need to use more."

—High school biology teacher

Using menus for enrichment and supplementary activities is the most common way of implementing menus in the classroom. Many teachers who want to "dip their toes" in the menu pool will begin by using menus this way because it does not directly impact their current teaching style. The students usually do not have much background knowledge, and information about the topic may not be readily available to all students while working on the menu.

When using menus for enrichment or supplemental activities, the teacher should introduce the menu and the choice activities at the beginning of a unit—before any instruction has taken place. The teacher then will progress through the content at the normal rate using their curricular materials, periodically allowing class and/or homework time throughout the unit for students to work on their menu choices to supplement a deeper understanding of the lessons being taught. Although it may seem counterintuitive to provide enrichment before any instruction takes place, it actually facilitates a need to know, or an epistemic curiosity (Litman et al., 2005).

This method incorporates an immediate use for the content the teacher is providing. For example, at the beginning of a unit, the teacher introduces the menu with the explanation that students may not have all of the knowledge to complete their choices yet. As instruction progresses, however, more content will be provided, and the students will be prepared to work on new choices. If students want to work ahead, they certainly can find the information on their own, but this is not required. Gifted students often see the ability to work ahead as a challenge and will begin to investigate concepts mentioned in the menu before the teacher has discussed them. Other students may start to develop questions about the concepts and then are ready to ask their questions when the teacher covers the new material. This "advance investigation" helps build an immense pool of background knowledge and potential content questions before the topic is even discussed in the classroom. As teachers, we constantly fight the battle of having students read ahead or "come to class prepared for discussion." By introducing a menu at the beginning of a unit and allowing students to complete products as instruction progresses, we encourage the students to naturally investigate the information and come to class prepared without having to make preparation a separate requirement.

Mainstream Instructional/Flipped Classroom Activities

"On your suggestion, I tried using the Game Show menu with my geometry unit since I had 3 days of instruction that the students knew well and could work on independently. They really responded to the independence."

—Secondary math teacher

Another option for using menus in the classroom is to offer a choice between certain in-class curricular activities. For example, after students have obtained basic instruction outside of the classroom (through research, videos, or other sources), students can be offered a menu of choices to organize their activities and facilitate their learning during class time. The students spend class time working on the activities on their menus; the teacher spends class time facilitating the choices that students have selected.

If teachers follow a more traditional model, menus can be used when students have some limited background knowledge about the content and appropriate information is readily available for them among their classroom resources. The teacher would select which aspects of the content must be directly taught to the students and which could be appropriately learned and reinforced through product menu activities. The unit is then designed using both formal instructional lessons and specific menu days during which the students will use the menu to strengthen the prior knowledge they already have learned, apply the new information, or extend recently presented information in a differentiated way. For this use of menus to be effective, the teacher must feel very comfortable with the students' prior knowledge level and their readiness to work independently.

Mini-Lessons

"I have so many different levels in my classroom, using menus with mini-lessons has been a life saver. I actually can work with small groups and everyone else doesn't run wild!"

—Secondary math teacher

Another option for menu use is the use of mini-lessons, with the menus driving the accompanying classroom activities. This method is best when most of the students have similar degrees of knowledge about the topic. The teacher designs short 10–15-minute mini-lessons, in which students quickly review fundamental concepts that already are familiar to them as well as experience new content in a brief, concise way. After these short mini-lessons, students can select an activity on the menu to demonstrate their understanding of the new concept.

The Game Show menu usually works well with mini-lessons. The menu can be designed so the topics across the top of the menu represent one mini-lesson per day (column). Using menus in this way shortens the amount of time teachers use the guided practice aspect of the lesson, so all instruction and examples should be carefully selected. The benefit of using menus with mini-lessons is the teacher gets to avoid the one-size-fits-all independent practice portion of the lesson. If a few students still struggle after the mini-lesson, they can be pulled into a small group while the other students work on their choices from the menu.

An important consideration when using menus this way is the independence level of the students. For mini-lesson menus to be effective, students will need to be able to work independently for up to 30 minutes after the mini-lesson. Students are often interested in the product they have chosen, so this may not be a critical issue, but it is still one worth mentioning as teachers consider how they would like to use various menus in their classroom.

Chapter 3

Guidelines for Products

"It was different being able to do something other than a drawing or folded paper. I haven't made a video for school in years!"

—High school chemistry student

This chapter outlines the different types of products used in the included menus as well as guidelines and expectations for each. It is crucial that students know the expectations of a product before they choose to work on it. By discussing these expectations before the students begin and having the information readily available, you will save frustration on everyone's part.

$1 Contract

"I really appreciate the $1 form. It kept me from having to run to [craft store] and spend $60 on felt and glitter and all of the other things we normally have to buy for projects."

—Parent of one of my students when asked for feedback on a recent menu

Consideration should be given to the cost of creating the products in any menu. The resources available to students vary within a classroom, and students should not be evaluated on the amount of materials they can purchase to make a product look glittery. The menus in this book are designed to equalize the resources students have available. For most products, the materials are available for under a dollar and can often be found in a teacher's classroom as part of their supplies. If a product would require materials from the student, the $1 contract is included as part of the product's guideline. This contract is an important aspect of the explanation of the product. By limiting the amount of money a child can spend, it creates an equality of resources for all students. This limitation also encourages a more creative product. When students are limited by the amount of materials they can readily purchase, they often have to use materials from home in new and unique ways. Figure 3.1 is a sample $1 contract that I have used many times with various products.

The Products

Table 3.1 contains a list of the products used in this book. These products were chosen for their flexibility in meeting learning preferences as well as being popular products most students have experienced and teachers may already use in their classroom. They have been arranged by learning preference—visual, kinesthetic, or auditory.

Each menu has been designed to include products from all of the learning preferences. Some of the products may be listed under more than one area depending on how they are presented or implemented (and some of the best products cross over between areas). The specific expectations (guidelines) for all of the products are presented in an easy-to-read card format that can be reproduced for students. This format is convenient for students to have in front of them when they work on their projects.

Product Frustrations

"One of the biggest reasons I haven't used more than one product at a time is that I have to constantly reexplain what I want for it. Even if the students write it down, it doesn't mean they won't pester me about it all week."

—English I teacher

$1 Contract

I did not spend more than $1.00 on my _____ .

_____   _____
            Student Signature   Date

My child, _____ , did not spend more than $1.00
on the product they created.

_____   _____
            Parent Signature   Date

Figure 3.1. $1 contract.

One of the biggest frustrations that accompany the use of a variety of menu products is the barrage of questions about the products themselves. Students can become so engulfed in the products and the criteria for creating them that they do not focus on the content being synthesized. This focus on products is especially true when menus are introduced to students.

Students can spend an exorbitant amount of time asking the teacher about the products mentioned on the menu. When this interrogation begins, what should have been a 10–15-minute menu introduction turns into 45–50 minutes of discussion about product expectations—without any discussion of the content!

During this discussion, teachers may consider showing students examples of the product(s) from the previous year. Although this can be helpful, it can also lead to additional frustration on the part of both the teacher and the students. Some students may not feel that they can produce a product as nice, as big, as special, or as (you fill in the blank) as the example. Alternatively, when shown an example, students might interpret that the teacher would like something exactly like the example they showed to students. To avoid this situation, I would propose that when using examples, students are shown a "blank" example that demonstrates how to create the shell of the product. For example, if a windowpane is needed, students might be shown a blank piece of paper that the teacher has divided into six panes. The students can then take the "skeleton" of

Table 3.1
Products

Visual	Kinesthetic	Auditory/Oral
Acrostic	Board Game	Board Game
Advertisement	Book Cover	Children's Book
Book Cover	Bulletin Board Display	Class Game
Brochure/Pamphlet	Card Sort	Classroom Model
Cartoon/Comic Strip	Class Game	Commercial
Children's Book	Classroom Model	Game Show
Choose Your Own	Collage	Interview
Adventure	Commercial	News Report
Collage	Concentration Cards	Play
Crossword Puzzle	Diorama	Presentation of Created
Diary/Journal	Flipbook	Product
Drawing	Foldable	PowerPoint–Speaker
Foldable	Folded Quiz Book	Puppet Show
Folded Quiz Book	Game Show	Speech
Graphic Novel	Mobile	Song/Rap
Greeting Card	Model	Student-Taught Lesson
Instruction Card	Mural	You Be the Person
Letter/Email	Museum Exhibit	Presentation
Map	Play	Video
Mind Map	Product Cube	
Newspaper Article	Puppet	
Poster	Quiz Board	
PowerPoint–Stand	Scrapbook	
Alone	Student-Taught Lesson	
Questionnaire	Three-Dimensional	
Quiz	Timeline	
Recipe	Trading Cards	
Scrapbook	Trophy	
Social Media Profile	Video	
Story	WebQuest	
Trading Cards		
Three Facts and a Fib		
Venn Diagram		
Visual Presentation/		
Product		
Webpage/Blog		
WebQuest		
Window Pane		
Worksheet		

the product and make it their own as they create their version of the windowpane using their information.

Product Guidelines

"Wow. You know how great these are . . . how much time they will save?"

—A group of teachers, when presented with a page of product guidelines for their classroom

Most frustrations associated with the varied products placed on menus can be addressed proactively using standardized, predetermined product guidelines. These guidelines should be shared with students prior to them creating any products. Although these guidelines may look like "mini-rubrics," they are designed in a generic way, such that any time throughout the school year that students select a product, that product's guidelines will apply.

A beneficial side effect of using set guidelines for a product is the security the guideline creates in the choice-making process. Students are often reticent to try something new, as doing so requires taking a risk. Traditionally, when students select products, they ask questions about creating the product, hope they remember all of the details, and submit the product for grading. It can be quite a shock when the students receive the product back and realize that their product was not complete or was not what the teacher expected. As you can imagine, students may not want to take the risk on something new the next time. Instead, they may prefer to stick to what they know and be successful. Using standardized product guidelines, students can begin to feel secure in their choice before they start working on a new product. Without this security, students tend to stay within their comfort zone.

Sharing the Product Guidelines

"Wow! It's already done for us."

—A group of teachers at staff development after
discovering the product guidelines pages

The guidelines for all of the products used on the menus in this book, as well as some potential free-choice options, are included in an easy-to-read card format (see Figure 3.2). Once the topic menu has been selected, there are many ways to share this information with students. There is no one "right way" to share the product guideline information with your students. The method you select depends on your students' abilities and needs.

For students who are independent and responsible (yes, they do exist!), teachers may duplicate and distribute all of the product guidelines pages to students at the beginning of the year. Students can glue them into the front of their notebooks or punch holes and place them in binders. By providing them in advance, each student has their copy to use while working on menu products during the school year.

If teachers prefer a more controlled method, class sets can be created. These sets can be created by gluing each product guideline onto a separate index card, hole punching the corner of each card, and placing all of the cards on a metal ring. These ring sets can be put in a central location or at a supply table where students can borrow and return them as they work on their products. Using a ring also allows for the addition of products as they are introduced. Additionally, the rings and index cards can be color-coded based on learning preference, encouraging students to step out of their comfort zone during free choice.

Some teachers prefer to expose students to products as students experience them on their menus. In this case, product guidelines from the menu currently assigned can be enlarged and posted on a bulletin board or wall for easy access during classroom work. Some teachers may choose to reproduce each menu's specific product guidelines on the back of the menu.

No matter which method teachers select to share the product guideline information with the students, teachers will save themselves a lot of time and frustration by having the product guidelines available for student reference (e.g., "Look at your product guidelines—I think that will answer your question").

Acrostic	Advertisement	Board Game
• Must be at least 8.5" by 11" • Must be neatly written or typed • Target word must be written down the left side of the paper • Each descriptive phrase chosen must begin with one of the letters from the target word • Each descriptive phrase chosen must be related to the target word • Name must be written on the acrostic	• Must be at least 8.5" by 11" • Must include a meaningful slogan • Must include a color picture of item or service • Must include price, if appropriate • Could be developed electronically • Name must be written on the advertisement	• Must have at least four thematic game pieces • Must have at least 25 colored/thematic squares • Must have at least 20 question/activity cards • Must have thematic title on the game • Must have a complete set of rules for playing the game • Must be at least the size of an open file folder • Name must be written on the front of the board game

Book Cover	Brochure/Pamphlet	Bulletin Board Display

Must include five parts:
• **Front cover**—title, author, image
• **Cover inside flap**—paragraph summary of the book
• **Back inside flap**—brief biography of author with at least five details
• **Back cover**—editorial comments about book
• **Spine**—title and author
  » May be placed on actual book, but not necessary
  » Name must be written on the book cover
	• Must be at least 8.5" by 11"
	• Must be in three-fold format
	• Front fold must have the title and picture
	• Must have both pictures and information
	• Information must be in paragraph form with at least five facts included
	• Bibliography or sources must be provided if needed
	• Can be created on computer
	• Any pictures from the Internet must have proper credit
	• Name must be written on the cover of the brochure
		• Must fit within assigned space on bulletin board or wall
		• Must include at least 10 details
		• Must have a title
		• Must have at least five different elements (posters, papers, questions, etc.)
		• Must have at least one interactive element that engages the reader
		• Name must be written on the bottom of the display

Card Sort	Cartoon/Comic Strip	Children's Book
• Must have at least 16 total cards • Must have at least five cards in each column • Can have more than two columns if appropriate • Answer key must be submitted • All cards must be submitted in a carrying bag • Name must be written on the carrying bag	• Must be at least 8.5" by 11" • Must have at least six cells • Must have meaningful dialogue that addresses the task • Must have color • Name must be written on the bottom of the cartoon or comic strip	• Must have a cover with book's title and student's name as author • Must have at least 10 pages • Each page must have an illustration to accompany the story • Must be neatly written or typed • Can be developed on the computer

Figure 3.2. Product guidelines.

Choose Your Own Adventure	Class Game	Classroom Model
• Must be neatly written or typed • Can be presented in an electronic format • Reader must be able to transition smoothly between choices • Readers must experience at least four choices in each story "strand" • Must include at least six unique endings • Must be appropriate length to allow for all of the adventures	• Game must allow all class members to participate • Must have only a few, easy-to-understand rules • Must be inventive or a new variation on a current game • Must have multiple question opportunities • Must provide answer key before the game is played • Name must be written on the answer key • The game must be approved by the teacher before being scheduled for play	• Must use everyone in the class in the model • Must not take longer than 2 minutes to arrange everyone • Students must be able to understand the part they play in the model • After the model is created, the explanation of the model must not take longer than 2 minutes • Must submit a paragraph that shares how the arrangement of students represents the concept being modeled • Name must be written on the paragraph submitted
Collage	**Commercial/Infomercial**	**Concentration Cards**
• Must be at least 8.5" by 11" • Pictures must be neatly cut from magazines or newspapers (no clip art) • Must label items as required in task • Name must be written on the bottom of the collage	• Must be between 1 and 3 minutes • Script must be turned in before commercial is presented • May be either live or recorded beforehand based on teacher discretion • Must have props or some form of costume(s) • Can include more than one person • Name must be written on the script	• Must have at least 20 index cards (10 matching sets) • Can use both pictures and words • Information must be placed on just one side of each card • Must include an answer key that shows the matches • All cards must be submitted in a carrying bag • Name must be written on the carrying bag
Cross Cut Model/Diagram	**Crossword Puzzle**	**Diary/Journal**
• Must include a scale to show the relationship between product and the actual item • Must include details about each layer • If creating a model, must also meet the criteria of a model • If creating a diagram, must also meet the criteria of a poster • Name must be written on the model	• Must have at least 20 significant words or phrases included • Clues must be appropriate • Must include puzzle and answer key • Can be created using a computer • Name must be written on the crossword puzzle	• Must be neatly written or typed • Must include the appropriate number of entries • Must include a date for each entry if appropriate • Must be written in first person • Name must be written on the diary or journal

Figure 3.2. Continued.

Diorama	Drawing	Essay
• Must be at least 4" by 5" by 8" • Must be self-standing • All interior space must be covered with relevant pictures and information • Name must be written on the back in permanent ink • Must submit a signed $1 contract • Informational/title card must be attached to diorama	• Must be at least 8.5" by 11" • Must show what is requested in the task statement • Must include color • Must be neatly drawn by hand • Must have title • Name must be written on the back	• Must be neatly written or typed • Must cover the specific topic in detail • Must be at least three paragraphs • Must include bibliography or sources if appropriate • Name must be written in the heading of the essay
Flipbook	**Foldable**	**Folded Quiz Book**
• Must be at least 8.5" by 11" folded in half • All information or opinions must be supported by facts • Must be created with the correct number of flaps cut into the top • Color is optional • Name must be written on the back of the flipbook	• At least 8.5" by 11" • The folds/design contribute to the information being shared • All information or opinion is complete and supported by facts • Color is optional • Name	• Must be at least 8.5" by 11" • Must have at least 10 questions • Must be created with the correct number of flaps cut into the top • Questions must be written or typed neatly on upper flaps • Answers must be written or typed neatly inside each flap • Color is optional • Name must be written on the back of the quiz book
Game Show	**Greeting Card**	**Instruction Card**
• Must have an emcee or host • Must have at least two contestants • Must have at least one regular round and a bonus round • Questions must be content specific • Props can be used, but are not mandatory • Name must be written on the questions used in the game	**Must include four parts:** • **Front**—colored pictures, words optional • **Front inside**—personal note related to topic • **Back inside**—greeting or saying, must meet menu task • **Back outside**—logo, publisher, and price for card » Name must be written on the back of the card	• Must be no larger than 5" by 8" • Must be created on heavy paper or card • Must be neatly written or typed • Must use color drawings • Must provide instructions stated in the task • Name must be written on the back of the card

Figure 3.2. Continued.

Interview	Letter/Email	Map
• Must have at least eight questions important to the topic being studied • Person chosen for interview must be an "expert" and qualified to provide answers based on product criteria • Questions and answers must be neatly written or typed • Name must be written on the interview questions	• Must be neatly written or typed • Must use proper letter format • Must have at least three paragraphs • Must follow type of letter stated in the menu (friendly, persuasive, informational) • Name must be included in the letter in a meaningful way	• Must be at least 8.5" by 11" • Must contain accurate information • Must include at least 10 relevant locations • Must include compass rose, legend, scale, key • Name must be written on the back of the map

Mind Map	Mobile	Model
• Must be at least 8.5" by 11" • Must use unlined paper • Must have one central idea • Must follow the "no more than four rule": There must be no more than four words coming from any one word • Must be neatly written or developed using a computer program • Name must be written on the mind map	• Must contain at least 10 pieces of related information • Must include color and pictures • Must include at least three layers of hanging information • Must be able to hang in a balanced way • Name must be written on one of the cards hanging from the mobile	• Must be at least 8" by 8" by 12" • Parts of model must be labeled • Must be in scale when appropriate • Must include a title card • Name must be permanently written on model

Mural	Museum Exhibit	News Report
• Must be at least 22" x 54" • Must have at least five pieces of important information • Must have colored pictures • Words are optional, but must have title • Name must be written on the back of the mural in a permanent way	• Must have title for exhibit • Must include at least five "artifacts" • Each artifact must be labeled with a neatly written card • Exhibit must fit within the size assigned • Must submit a signed $1 contract • No expensive or irreplaceable objects may be used in the display • Name must be written on a label card in the exhibit	• Must address the who, what, where, when, why, and how of the topic • Script of news report must be turned in with product, or before if performance will be "live" • May be either live or recorded beforehand based on teacher discretion • Name announced during the performance and clearly written on script

Figure 3.2. Continued.

Newspaper Article	Play/Skit	Poster
• Must be informational in nature • Must follow standard newspaper format • Must include picture with caption that supports article • Must contain at least three paragraphs • Must be neatly written or typed • Name must be written at the top of the article	• Must be between 3 and 5 minutes • Script must be turned in before play is presented • May be presented to an audience or recorded for future showing to audience based on teacher discretion • Must have props or some form of costume • Can include more than one person • Name must be written on the script that is submitted with the play	• Must be the size of a standard poster board • Must contain at least five pieces of important information • Must have title • Must have both words and pictures • Name must be written on the back of the poster in a permanent way • Bibliography or sources must be included as needed

PowerPoint–Stand Alone	PowerPoint–Speaker	Project Cube
• Must contain at least 10 informational slides • Must not have more than 10 words per page • Slides must have color and no more than one graphic per page • Animations are optional but must not distract from the information being presented • Bibliography or sources must be included as needed • Name must be written on the first slide of the PowerPoint	• Must contain at least 10 informational slides • Must not have more than two words per page • Slides must have color and no more than one graphic per page • Animations are optional but must not distract from information being presented • Presentation must be timed and flow with the speech being given • Name must be written on the first slide of the PowerPoint	• All six sides of the cube must be filled with information as stated in the task • Must be neatly written or typed • Name must be printed neatly on the bottom of one of the sides of the cube • Must be submitted flat for grading

Puppet	Questionnaire	Quiz
• Puppet must be handmade and must have a movable mouth • A list of supplies used to make the puppet must be turned in with the puppet • Must submit a signed $1 contract • If used in a puppet show, all play criteria must be met as well • Name must be written on the inside of the puppet where it can be seen	• Must be neatly written or typed • Must contain at least 10 questions with possible answers • Must contain at least one answer that requires a written response • Questions must be helpful to gathering information on the topic begin studied • If questionnaire is to be used, at least 15 people must provide answers • Name must be written at the top of the questionnaire	• Must be at least a half sheet of paper • Must be neatly written or typed • Must cover the specific topic in detail • Must include at least five questions, including at least one short answer question • Must have at least one graphic • An answer key must be turned in with the quiz • Name must be written on the top of the quiz

Figure 3.2. Continued.

Quiz Board	Recipe/Recipe Card	Scrapbook
• Must have at least five questions • Must have at least five answers, although there could be more for distractors • Must use a system with lights to facilitate self-checking • Name must be written in a permanent way on the back of the quiz board	• Must be written neatly or typed on a piece of paper or an index card • Must have a list of ingredients with measurements for each • Must have numbered steps that explain how to make the recipe • Name must be written at the top of the recipe card	• Cover of scrapbook must have a meaningful title and student's name • Must have at least five themed pages • Each page must have at least one meaningful picture • All photos and pictures must have captions • Bibliography or sources must be included as needed
Social Media Profile	**Song/Rap**	**Speech**
• Must include profile picture • Must include other relevant information about the "person" • Must include at least five status updates with comments from "friends" • Can be created electronically or in poster format • Name must be included on the social media profile in a creative way	• Must be original (not found online or sung by anyone else before) • Words or lyrics must make sense • May be either live or recorded beforehand based on teacher discretion • Written words must be turned in before performance or with taped song • Must be at least 2 minutes in length • Name must be written on the written words submitted with the song or rap	• Must be at least 2 minutes in length • Must not be read from written paper • Note cards can be used • Written speech must be turned in before speech is presented • May be either live or recorded beforehand based on teacher discretion • Voice must be clear, loud, and easy to understand • Name must be written on the written speech
Story	**Three-Dimensional Timeline**	**Three Facts and a Fib**
• Must be neatly written or typed • Must have all elements of a well-written story (setting, characters, conflict, rising action, and resolution) • Must be appropriate length to allow for story elements • Name must be written on the story	• Must not be bigger than a standard-size poster board • Must be divided into equal time units • Must contain at least 10 important dates • Must have at least two sentences explaining why each date is important • Must have a meaningful object securely attached beside each date to represent that date • Objects must be creative • Must be able to explain how each object represents each date or event • Name must be written at the bottom of the timeline	• Can be handwritten, typed, or created in PowerPoint • Must include exactly four statements: three true statements (facts) and one false statement (fib) • False statement must not be obvious • Brief paragraph must accompany product that explains why the fib is false • Name must be written on the product

Figure 3.2. Continued.

Trading Cards	Trophy	Venn Diagram
• Must include at least 10 cards • Each card must be at least 3" by 5" • Each card must have a colored picture • Must contain at least three facts on the subject of the card • Cards must have information on both sides • All cards must be submitted in a carrying bag • Name must be written on the carrying bag	• Must be at least 6" tall • Must have a base with the name of the person getting the trophy and the name of the award written neatly or typed on it • Top of trophy must be appropriate and represent the nature of the award • Name must be written on the bottom of the award • Must be an original trophy (avoid reusing a trophy from home)	• Must be at least 8.5" by 11" • Diagram shapes must be thematic (rather than just circles) and neatly drawn • Must have a title for entire diagram and a title for each section • Must have at least six items in each section of the diagram • Name must be written neatly on the back of the paper
Video	Visual Presentation/Product	WebQuest
• Must use video format • Must submit a written plan or story board with project • Students must arrange their own way to record their video or allow teacher at least 3 days notice for help in obtaining a way to record the video • Must cover pertinent information • Name must be written on the label or in the file name	This product may be a: • Poster • Cartoon • PowerPoint (or similar tool) • Video • Bulletin Board Display • Other product with free choice proposal form • Please read the guidelines specific to your choice	• Must quest through at least five high-quality websites • Websites must be linked in the document • Can be submitted using a word processor or PowerPoint • Must contain at least three questions for each website • Must address the topic • Name must be written on the WebQuest or in the file name
Webpage/Blog	Window Pane	Worksheet
• Words are neat and easy to read without distractions • Must cover the specific topic in detail • Must be at least three paragraphs and include links to at least three relevant resources • Must include bibliography or sources when appropriate at the bottom of the page	• Must be at least 8.5" by 11" on unlined paper • Must contain at least six squares • Each square must include both a picture and words • All pictures must be both creative and meaningful • Must be neatly written or typed • Name must be written on the bottom right-hand corner of the front of the window pane	• Must be 8.5" by 11" • Must be neatly written or typed • Must cover the specific topic or question in detail • Must be creative in design • Must have at least one graphic • An answer key must be turned in with the worksheet • Name must be written at the top of the worksheet

Figure 3.2. Continued.

You Be the Person Presentation		
• Presenter must take on the role of the person • Must cover at least five important facts about the life or achievements of the person • Must be between 2 and 4 minutes in length • Script must be turned in before information is presented • Must be presented to an audience with the ability to answer questions while in character • Must have props or some form of costume • Name must be written on the script		

Figure 3.2. Continued.

CHAPTER 4

Rubrics

"One rubric—and I can grade everything? Now we are talking!"

—Group of secondary teachers

The most common reason teachers feel uncomfortable with menus is the need for fair and equal grading. If all of the students create the same product, teachers feel these products are easier to grade than 100 different products, none of which looks like any other. The great equalizer for hundreds of different products is a generic rubric that can evaluate the important qualities of an excellent product.

All-Purpose Rubric

Figure 4.1 is an example of a rubric that has been classroom tested with various menus. This rubric can be used with any point value activity presented in a menu, as there are five criteria, and the columns represent full points, half points, and no points. For example, if a student completes a 20-point product, each criterion would be worth four points (full

All-Purpose Rubric

Name: _____

Criteria	Excellent (Full Credit)	Good (Half Credit)	Poor (No Credit)	Self
Content Is the content of the product well chosen?	Content chosen represents the best choice for the product. Information or graphics are well chosen and related to content.	Information or graphics are related to content, but are not the best choice for the product.	Information or graphics present do not appear related to the topic or task.	
Completeness Is everything included in the product?	All information needed is included. Product meets the product guideline criteria and the criteria of the menu task.	Some important information is missing. Product meets the product guideline criteria and the criteria of the menu task.	Most important information is missing. The product does not meet the task or does not meet the product criteria.	
Creativity Is the product original?	Presentation of information is from a new and original perspective. Graphics are original. Product includes elements of fun and interest.	Presentation of information is from a new perspective. Graphics are not original. Product has elements of fun and interest.	There is no evidence of new thoughts or perspectives in the product, or any part of the product was plagiarized.	
Correctness Is all of the information included correct?	All information presented is correct and accurate.		Any portion of the information presented in product is incorrect.	
Communication Is the information in the product well communicated?	All information is neat and easy to read. Product is in appropriate format and shows significant effort. Oral presentation was easy to understand and presented with fluency.	Most (80%) of the product is neat and easy to read. Product is in appropriate format and shows significant effort. Oral presentation was easy to understand, with some fluency.	More than 20% of the product is not neat and easy to read, or the product is not in the appropriate format. It does not show significant effort. Oral presentation was not fluent or easy to understand.	
			Total Grade:	

Figure 4.1. All-purpose rubric.

points), two points (half points), and zero (no points). Although Tic-Tac-Toe and Meal menus are not point based, this rubric can also be used to grade products from these menus. Teachers simply assign 100 points to each of the three products on the Tic-Tac-Toe and Meal menus. Then each criterion would be worth 20 points, and the all-purpose rubric can be used to grade each product individually.

There are different ways that teachers can share this rubric with students. Some teachers prefer to provide it when they present a menu to students. The rubric can be reproduced on the back of the menu along with its guidelines. The rubric can also be given to students at the beginning of the year with the product guideline cards. This way, students will always know the expectations as they complete projects throughout the school year. Some teachers prefer to keep a master copy of the rubric for themselves and post an enlarged copy on a bulletin board. If teachers wanted to share the rubric with parents, they could provide a copy for parents during back-to-school night, open house, or on private teacher web pages so that the parents will understand how teachers will grade their children's products.

No matter how teachers choose to share the rubric with students, the first time students see this rubric, it should be explained in detail, especially the last column, titled "Self." It is imperative that students self-evaluate their products. The Self column can provide a unique perspective on the product as it is being graded. *Note*: This rubric was designed to be specific enough that students will understand the criteria the teacher is seeking, but general enough that they can still be as creative as they like in the creation of their product.

Student-Taught Lessons and Student Presentation Rubrics

Although the all-purpose rubric can be used for all of the activities included on the menus in this book, there are two occasions that seem to warrant a special rubric: student-taught lessons and student presentations. These are unique situations, with many fine details that must be considered to create a quality product.

Student-taught lessons are a unique situation. School curricula are already packed with information and teachers often feel that turning class time over to students should only be done if the experience will benefit everyone involved. Teachers would like to allow students to teach their classmates but are concerned about quality lessons and may not comfortable with the grading aspect of the assignment. Rarely do students understand all of the components that go into designing an effective lesson. This student-taught lesson rubric (see Figure 4.2) helps focus students on the important aspects of a well-designed lesson and allows teachers to make the evaluation a little more subjective.

Student presentations can be difficult to evaluate. The first consideration with these types of presentations is objectivity. Objectivity can be addressed through a specific presentation rubric that reinforces the expectations for the speaker. The rubric will need to be discussed and various criteria demonstrated before the students begin preparing their presentations. The second consideration is that of the audience and their interest in the presentation. How frustrating is it to have to grade 30 presentations when the audience is not paying attention, off task, or tuning out? This issue can be solved by allowing your audience to be directly involved in the presentation by providing them a rubric that can be used to provide feedback to their classmates. If all students have been instructed on the student presentation rubric (see Figure 4.3), when they receive their feedback rubric, they will be quite comfortable with the criteria. During this process, students are asked to rank their classmates on a scale of 1–10 in the areas of content, flow, and the prop they chose to enhance their presentation. Additionally, students are asked to state two things the presenter did well.

Although most students understand this should be a positive experience for the presenter, it may need to be reinforced that certain types of feedback are not necessary; for example, if the presenter dropped their prop and had to pick it up, the presenter knows this and it probably does not need to be told again. The feedback should be positive and specific as well. A comment of "Great!" is not what should be recorded; instead, something specific such as, "You spoke loudly and clearly" or "You used great sources!" should be written on the form. These types of comments really make the students take note and feel great about their presentations. The teacher should not be surprised to note that the students often look through all of their classmates' feedback and comments before ever consulting the rubric the teacher completed. Once students have completed a feedback form for a presenter, the forms can then be gathered at the end of each presentation, stapled together, and given to the presenter at the end of the class.

Student-Taught Lesson Rubric

Name: _____

Parts of Lesson	Excellent	Good	Fair	Poor	Self
Prepared and Ready All materials and lesson ready at the start of class period, from warm-up to conclusion of lesson.	10 Everything is ready to present.	6 Lesson is present, but small amount of scrambling.	3 Lesson is present, but major scrambling.	0 No lesson ready or missing major components.	
Understanding Presenter(s) understands the material well. Students understand information presented.	20 All information is correct and in correct format.	12 Presenter understands; 25% of students do not.	4 Presenter understands; 50% of students do not.	0 Presenter is confused.	
Complete Includes all significant information from section or topic.	15 Includes all important information.	10 Includes most important information.	2 Includes less than 50% of the important information.	0 Information is not related.	
Practice Includes some way for students to practice the information presented.	20 Practice present; was well chosen.	10 Practice present; can be applied effectively.	5 Practice present; not related or best choice.	0 No practice or students are confused.	
Interest/Fun Most of the class was involved, interested, and participating.	15 Everyone interested and participating.	10 75% actively participating.	5 Less than 50% actively participating.	0 Everyone off task.	
Creativity Information presented in an imaginative way.	20 Wow, creative! I never would have thought of that!	12 Good ideas!	5 Some good pieces but general instruction.	0 No creativity; all lecture, notes, or worksheet.	

Your Topic/Objective:

Comments:

Don't forget: All copy requests and material requests must be made at least 24 hours in advance.

Figure 4.2. Student-taught lesson rubric.

Oral Presentation Rubric

Name: _____

	Excellent	Good	Fair	Poor	Self
Content–Complete The presentation included everything it should.	**30** Presentation included all of the important information about the math topic being presented.	**20** Presentation covered most of the important information, but one key idea was missing.	**10** Presentation covered some of the important information, but more than one key idea was missing.	**0** Presentation included some information, but it was trivial or fluff.	
Content–Correct All of the information presented was accurate.	**30** All of the information presented was accurate. Presenter clearly understood the information presented.	**20** All information presented was correct with a few unintentional errors that were quickly corrected.		**0** The information presented was not correct.	
Content–Consistency Presenter stayed on topic during the presentation.	**10** Presenter stayed on topic 100% of the time.	**7** Presenter stayed on topic 90–99% of the time.	**4** Presenter stayed on topic 80–89% of the time.	**0** It was hard to tell what the topic was.	
Prop Presenter had at least one prop that was directly related to the presentation.	20 Presenter had the prop to help illustrate the math concept, and it complimented the presentation.	12 Presenter had a prop, but it was not the best choice.	4 Presenter had a prop, but there was no clear reason for its choice.	0 No prop present.	
Flow Presenter knew the presentation well, so the words were well-spoken and flowed well together.	10 Presentation flowed well. Speaker did not stumble over words.	7 Some flow problems, but they did not distract from information.	4 Some flow problems interrupted presentation; presenter seemed flustered.	0 Constant flow problems; information was not presented in a way it could be understood.	
			Total Grade:		

Figure 4.3. Oral presentation rubric.

PART II

The Menus

How to Use the Menu Pages

Each menu in this section has:
- an introduction page for the teacher,
- the content menu, and
- any specific activities mentioned in the menu.

Introduction Pages

The introduction pages are meant to provide an overview of each menu. They are divided into five areas.
- *Objectives Covered Through the Menu and Activities.* This area will list all of the insutrctional objectives that the menu can address. Although all of the objectives integrated into the menus correlate to state and national standards, these targets will be stated in a generic, teacher-friendly way. Menus are arranged in such a way that if students complete the guidelines outlined in the instructions for the menu, all of these objectives will be covered.

- *Materials Needed by Students for Completion.* For each menu, it is expected that the teacher will provide, or students will have access to, the following materials:
  - lined paper,
  - blank 8.5" by 11" white paper,
  - large white paper or poster board,
  - glue, and
  - colored pencils or markers.

The introduction page also includes a list of additional materials that may be needed by students as they complete the menu. Students do have the choice of the menu items they can complete, so it is possible that the teacher will not need all of these materials for every student.

- *Special Notes on the Use of This Menu.* Some menus allow students to choose to present products to their classmates, build items out of recycled materials, or build quiz boards. This section will outline any special tips on managing products that may require more time, supplies, or space. This section will also share any tips to consider for a particular activity.
- *Time Frame.* Each menu has its ideal time frame based on its structure, but all need at least one week to complete. Menus that assess more objectives are better suited to more than 2 weeks. This section will give you an overview of the best time frame for completing the entire menu, as well as options for shorter time periods. If teachers do not have time to devote to a whole menu, they certainly can choose the 1–2-day option for any menu topic students are currently studying.
- *Suggested Forms.* This section contains a list of the rubrics or forms that should be available for students as the menus are introduced. If a menu has a free-choice option, the appropriate proposal form also will be listed here.

CHAPTER 5

The New World

The New World

Tic-Tac-Toe Menu

Objectives Covered Through This Menu and These Activities
- Students will understand the impact of geographic factors on Native Americans in various geographical locations.
- Students will create written, oral, and visual presentations of social studies information using effective communication skills, including proper citations and avoiding plagiarism.
- Students will use social studies terminology correctly.

Materials Needed by Students for Completion
- Poster board or large white paper
- Blank index cards (for card sorts)
- Recording software or application (for songs)
- Graph paper or Internet access (for WebQuests)

Special Notes on the Use of This Menu
- This menu allows students to create a WebQuest. There are multiple versions and templates for WebQuests available on the Internet. It is your decision whether you would like to specify a format or if you will allow students to create one of their own choosing.

Time Frame
- 2–3 weeks—Students are given the menu as the unit is started. The teacher will go over all of the options for that content and have students place checkmarks in the boxes that represent the activities they are most interested in completing. As students choose activities, they should complete a column or a row. When students complete this pattern, they have completed one activity from each content area, learning style, or level of Bloom's revised taxonomy, depending on the design of the menu. As the teacher presents lessons throughout the week, they should refer back to the menu options associated with that content.
- 1 week—At the start of the unit, the teacher chooses the three activities they feel are most valuable for students. Stations can be set up in

the classroom. These three activities are available for student choice throughout the week as regular instruction takes place.
- 1–2 days—The teacher chooses an activity from the menu to use with the entire class.

Suggested Forms
- All-purpose rubric
- Free-choice proposal form
- Presentation rubric

Name:_____ Date:_____

The New World

Directions: In this menu you will need to address each of the following regions at least once through your products. Use the following checklist to be sure you have addressed all of the regions. Then, check the boxes for the products you plan to complete. They should form a tic-tac-toe across or down. All products are due by: _____ .

❑ Pacific Northwest ❑ The Great Plains ❑ Eastern Woodlands
❑ Desert Southwest ❑ The Great Basin ❑ _____

❑ *Native Americans* Research two groups of Native Americans that lived in two different regions. Prepare a social media profile for an individual who lives in each area.	❑ *Climate* Write Three Facts and a Fib about the climate of one of the regions and its impact on the Native Americans who lived in that area.	❑ *Resources* Develop a quiz to test your classmates' knowledge of the different resources found in no more than two different regions.
❑ *Resources* Write a Choose Your Own Adventure story set in the 1400s in which the reader has to make life decisions based on the resources found in one of the regions.	❑ **Free Choice: Native Americans** (Fill out your proposal form before beginning the free choice!)	❑ *Climate* Create a card sort that others could use to classify aspects of two different regions. Be sure to include how these aspects impacted the lives of those who lived in that area.
❑ *Climate* Make a Venn diagram to compare and contrast the climates (and their impacts) of at least two different regions.	❑ *Resources* Prepare a WebQuest about the different resources found in one of the regions and how different Native Americans used those resources.	❑ *Native Americans* Write and record an original song that helps others understand the lives of one specific group of Native Americans (check off the region for this group).

The Columbian Exchange

20-50-80 Menu

Objectives Covered Through This Menu and These Activities

- Students will analyze various aspects of the Columbian Exchange.
- Students will discuss the political, economic, and social events and issues related to the Columbian Exchange.
- Students will create written, oral, and visual presentations of social studies information using effective communication skills, including proper citations and avoiding plagiarism.
- Students will analyze information by applying absolute and relative chronology.
- Students will use social studies terminology correctly.

Materials Needed by Students for Completion

- Poster board or large white paper
- Recycled materials (for models)
- Graph paper or Internet access (for WebQuests)
- Materials for three-dimensional timelines
- Recording software or application (for videos)

Special Notes on the Use of This Menu

- This menu gives students the opportunity to create a video. The grading and sharing of these products can often be facilitated by having students prerecord their product using whatever technology is most convenient for the teacher. This allows the teacher to decide when it will be shown as well as keeps the presentation to its intended length. If recording options are limited, this activity can be modified by allowing students to act out the product (like a play) in front of the class.
- This menu asks students to use recycled materials to create their model. This does not mean only plastic and paper; instead, students should focus on using materials in new ways. It works well if a box is started for "recycled" contributions at the beginning of the school year. That way, students always have access to these types of materials.
- This menu allows students to create a WebQuest. There are multiple versions and templates for WebQuests available on the Internet. It is

your decision whether you would like to specify a format or if you will allow students to create one of their own choosing.

Time Frame

- 1–2 weeks—Students are given a menu as the unit is started, and the teacher discusses all of the product options on the menu. As the different options are discussed, students will choose the activities they are most interested in completing so that they meet their goal of 100 points. As the lessons progress through the week(s), the teacher and students refer back to the menu options associated with the content being taught.
- 1–2 days—The teacher chooses an activity or product from the menu to use with the entire class.

Suggested Forms

- All-purpose rubric
- Proposal form for point-based projects
- Presentation rubric

Name:_____ Date:_____

The Columbian Exchange

Directions: Choose at least two activities from the menu below. The activities must total 100 points. Place a checkmark next to each box to show which activities you will complete. All activities must be completed by _____ .

---

20 Points

- ❒ Make a T-chart that shares the benefits and consequences of the Columbian Exchange.

- ❒ Create a foldable that could be used to illustrate the details of the Columbian Exchange.

---

50 Points

- ❒ After examining the mechanisms of the Columbian Exchange, prepare a model that demonstrates how the Columbian Exchange progressed from the 1500s to the 1700s.

- ❒ When different cultures interact, each impacts the other in different ways. Assemble a WebQuest to show how Native Americans and English settlers impacted each other in both positive and negative ways during this time period.

- ❒ Build a three-dimensional timeline that shows the events leading up to and following the Columbian Exchange. Use your timeline to demonstrate its impact on the world.

- ❒ **Free choice on the impacts of the Columbian Exchange on different stakeholders**—Prepare a proposal form and submit it to your teacher for approval.

---

80 Points

- ❒ After investigating the impact of the Columbian Exchange on all stakeholders, prepare and share a realistic written plan that could have been implemented to eliminate (or at least reduce) the negative impacts on Native Americans.

- ❒ Consider the causes and effects of the Columbian Exchange as whole. Based on your views, identify another similar event that has occurred anytime between the Columbian Exchange and today. Record a video to draw analogies between the Columbian Exchange and the event you selected.

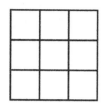

The Colonies and the Growth of Slavery

Tic-Tac-Toe Menu

Objectives Covered Through This Menu and These Activities
- Students will explain how indentured servants impacted the colonies.
- Students will investigate events that lead to the rise of slavery.
- Students will describe plantation life in different colonies.
- Students will create written, oral, and visual presentations of social studies information using effective communication skills, including proper citations and avoiding plagiarism.
- Students will use a variety of rich primary and secondary source material.
- Students will identify bias and support with historical evidence.
- Students will analyze information by applying absolute and relative chronology.
- Students will use social studies terminology correctly.

Materials Needed by Students for Completion
- Poster board or large white paper
- Magazines (for collages)
- Recycled materials (for museum exhibit)
- Blank index cards (for trading cards)
- Recording software or application (for documentary)

Special Notes on the Use of This Menu
- This menu gives students the opportunity to create a documentary. The grading and sharing of these products can often be facilitated by having students prerecord their product using whatever technology is most convenient for the teacher. This allows the teacher to decide when it will be shown as well as keeps the presentation to its intended length. If recording options are limited, this activity can be modified by allowing students to act out the product (like a play) in front of the class.
- This menu asks students to use recycled materials to create their museum exhibit. This does not mean only plastic and paper; instead, students should focus on using materials in new ways. It works well

if a box is started for "recycled" contributions at the beginning of the school year. That way, students always have access to these types of materials.

Time Frame

- 2–3 weeks—Students are given the menu as the unit is started. The teacher will go over all of the options for that content and have students place checkmarks in the boxes that represent the activities they are most interested in completing. As students choose activities, they should complete a column or a row. When students complete this pattern, they have completed one activity from each content area, learning style, or level of Bloom's revised taxonomy, depending on the design of the menu. As the teacher presents lessons throughout the week, they should refer back to the menu options associated with that content.
- 1 week—At the start of the unit, the teacher chooses the three activities they feel are most valuable for students. Stations can be set up in the classroom. These three activities are available for student choice throughout the week as regular instruction takes place.
- 1–2 days—The teacher chooses an activity from the menu to use with the entire class.

Suggested Forms

- All-purpose rubric
- Free-choice proposal form
- Presentation rubric

The Colonies and the Growth of Slavery

Directions: Check the boxes you plan to complete. They should form a tic-tac-toe across or down. All products are due by: _____ .

☐ *Plantation Life*	☐ *Growth of Slavery*	☐ *Indentured Servants*
Design a collage that shares how the growing of different types of crops impacted plantations in the colonies.	Build a museum exhibit that could be used to share how the Stono Rebellion contributed to the growth of slavery.	Make a mind map that organizes pertinent information about the indentured servant process.
☐ *Indentured Servants*	☐ **Free Choice: Plantation Life** (Fill out your proposal form before beginning the free choice!)	☐ *Growth of Slavery*
Draw a truthful yet enticing advertisement that may have been used to recruit indentured servants.		Assemble a set of trading cards for primary and secondary sources that document the different economic, social, and geographical factors that impacted the growth of slavery.
☐ *Growth of Slavery*	☐ *Indentured Servants*	☐ *Plantation Life*
Record a documentary about Bacon's Rebellion and its impact on the growth of slavery. Include unbiased views from each side of the rebellion.	Write an editorial newspaper article that opines the impact of removing the headright system.	Prepare Three Facts and a Fib about how geography impacted the economics of plantations.

Religious Persecution

Topic List Menu

Objectives Covered Through This Menu and These Activities

- Students will examine Puritan and Quaker beliefs.
- Students will determine the impact of historical figures.
- Students will discuss the political, economic, and social events and issues related to religious groups in colonial America.
- Students will create written, oral, and visual presentations of social studies information using effective communication skills, including proper citations and avoiding plagiarism.
- Students will analyze information by applying absolute and relative chronology.
- Students will use social studies terminology correctly.
- Students will examine the impact of geographic factors on major events.

Materials Needed by Students for Completion

- Poster board or large white paper
- Blank index cards (for card sorts, trading cards)
- Recording software or application (for commercials, videos)
- Graph paper or Internet access (for WebQuests)

Special Notes on the Use of This Menu

- This menu gives students the opportunity to create a video. The grading and sharing of these products can often be facilitated by having students prerecord their product using whatever technology is most convenient for the teacher. This allows the teacher to decide when it will be shown as well as keeps the presentation to its intended length. If recording options are limited, this activity can be modified by allowing students to act out the product (like a play) in front of the class.
- This menu gives students the opportunity to teach a concept. This can take a significant amount of time and organization. It can save time if the students who choose to do a lesson can sign up for a designated day and time that is determined when the menu is distributed.
- This menu allows students to create a WebQuest. There are multiple versions and templates for WebQuests available on the Internet. It is

your decision whether you would like to specify a format or if you will allow students to create one of their own choosing.

- This menu gives students the opportunity to facilitate a class game. The expectation is that all students in the classroom will play an active role in the game. This may mean that the facilitator may need some additional space and time for their game. This can take a significant amount of time and organization. It can save time if all of the students who choose to present their game can sign up for a designated day and time that is determined when the menu is distributed.

- This menu provides the students the option of creating a visual presentation or product. This term has been included on the product guidelines, but it refers to students having a choice of what type of visual product they would like to create. On the product guidelines, they will find a short list, but they are welcome to propose other web-based or tangible options.

Time Frame

- 1–2 weeks—Students are given the menu as the unit is started, and the guidelines and point expectations are discussed. Students usually will need to earn 100 points for 100%, although there is an opportunity for extra credit if the teacher would like to use another target number. Because this menu covers one topic in depth, the teacher will go over all of the options for the topic being covered and have students place checkmarks in the boxes next to the activities they are most interested in completing. Teachers will need to set aside a few moments to sign the agreement at the bottom of the page with each student. As instruction continues, activities are completed by students and submitted to the teacher for grading.

- 1–2 days—The teacher chooses an activity or product from an objective to use with the entire class during that lesson time.

Suggested Forms

- All-purpose rubric
- Proposal form for point-based products
- Presentation rubric

Name:_____ Date:_____

Religious Persecution

Guidelines:

1. You may complete as many of the activities listed as you wish within the time period.
2. You may choose any combination of activities, but **must** complete at least one activity from each topic area.
3. Your goal is 100 points. (This is a grade of 100/100.) You may earn up to _____ points extra credit.
4. You may be as creative as you like within the guidelines listed below.
5. You must show your plan to your teacher by _____ .
6. Activities may be turned in at any time during the working time period. They will be graded and recorded on this sheet as you continue to work, so keep it safe!

Topic	Plan to Do	Activity to Complete	Point Value	Date Completed	Points Earned
Religious Beliefs		Assemble a card sort of Christian, Puritan, and Quaker beliefs.	15		
		Draw two outlines of people, and label at least seven different body parts on each as they relate to Puritan and Quaker beliefs.	20		
		Create a Venn diagram to compare the relationships between the Native Americans, Quakers, and Puritans.	20		
		You are a teenage Puritan. Write three journal entries about your life in the colonies. Include one entry about an encounter with a Quaker teenager.	25		
		Consider the reasons behind the Puritans' immigration and their beliefs about diversity. Record a speech in which you address these topics.	30		
Historical Figures		Design a set of trading cards for historical figures associated with the Quakers and Puritans.	15		
		Read John Winthrop's famous speech about his city upon a hill. Select at least two quotes from the speech and illustrate them in a visual product.	20		
		William Penn used an advertising campaign to attract movement to Pennsylvania. Write a commercial he would have used.	25		
		Create a social media profile for Anne Hutchinson. Her friends must include at least one other historical figure from each century.	25		
		Record a video in which you are Roger Williams looking into the future. Share the reasons for your actions and your possible impact on history.	30		
Influential Factors		Draw a mind map to outline the societal factors that caused actions from Quakers and Puritans.	15		
		Create a poster that shows the different geographical and economic factors that impacted the Quakers and Puritans.	20		
		Brainstorm a class game in which your classmates answer questions from the perspective of a Quaker or a Puritan about factors that impact their lives.	25		
		Considering the push factors that impacted Puritans and Quakers, identify at least two other groups in history who have responded similarly. Prepare a WebQuest to show the parallels between the all of the groups.	30		
Any		**Free Choice:** Submit your free-choice proposal form for a product of your choice.			
		Total number of points you are planning to earn.		Total points earned:	

I am planning to complete _____ activities that could earn up to a total of _____ points.

Teacher's initials _____ Student's signature _____

20 Points
□ _____
□ _____
□ _____
50 Points
□ _____
□ _____
□ _____
□ _____
80 Points
□ _____
□ _____

The First Great Awakening

20-50-80 Menu

Objectives Covered Through This Menu and These Activities

- Students will discuss the political, economic, and social events and issues related to the First Great Awakening.
- Students will create visual representations of historical information.
- Students will analyze information by applying absolute and relative chronology.
- Students will apply the process of historical inquiry to research, interpret, and use multiple types of sources of evidence.
- Students will describe the relationship between the arts and popular culture and the times during which they were created.
- Students will describe how the characteristics of and issues in U.S. history have been reflected in various genres of art, music, film, and literature.
- Students will examine the impact of geographic factors on major events.

Materials Needed by Students for Completion

- Poster board or large white paper
- Materials for three-dimensional timelines
- Recording software or application (for videos)

Special Notes on the Use of This Menu

- This menu gives students the opportunity to create a video. The grading and sharing of these products can often be facilitated by having students prerecord their product using whatever technology is most convenient for the teacher. This allows the teacher to decide when it will be shown as well as keeps the presentation to its intended length. If recording options are limited, this activity can be modified by allowing students to act out the product (like a play) in front of the class.
- This menu gives students the opportunity to facilitate a class model. The expectation is that all students in the classroom will play an active role in the model. This may mean that students need some additional space for their model.

- This menu provides the students the option of creating a visual presentation or product. This term has been included on the product guidelines, but it refers to students having a choice of what type of visual product they would like to create. On the product guidelines, they will find a short list, but they are welcome to propose other web-based or tangible options.

Time Frame

- 1–2 weeks—Students are given a menu as the unit is started, and the teacher discusses all of the product options on the menu. As the different options are discussed, students will choose the activities they are most interested in completing so that they meet their goal of 100 points. As the lessons progress through the week(s), the teacher and students refer back to the menu options associated with the content being taught.
- 1–2 days—The teacher chooses an activity or product from the menu to use with the entire class.

Suggested Forms

- All-purpose rubric
- Proposal form for point-based projects
- Presentation rubric

The First Great Awakening

Directions: Choose at least two activities from the menu below. The activities must total 100 points. Place a checkmark next to each box to show which activities you will complete. All activities must be completed by _____ .

---

20 Points

❏ Create a Venn diagram to compare New and Old Light ministers.

❏ Build a three-dimensional timeline that details the events of the First Great Awakening.

---

50 Points

❏ Consider the qualities of New and Old Light ministers. Make a T-chart of ministers through history who represent each view. Include a short defense for each selection.

❏ Develop a class model that demonstrates the different impacts of the events of the First Great Awakening.

❏ Prepare a visual presentation to share how the Great Awakening influenced artists. Include a brief description for each example.

❏ **Free choice on the societal impacts of the First Great Awakening—** Prepare a proposal form and submit it to your teacher for approval.

---

80 Points

❏ Write a Choose Your Own Adventure story about a new minister selecting their religious path.

❏ The First Great Awakening impacted many different groups of people. Record a video in which you interview (fictitious) people from different groups who are impacted by the social and political aspects of this event.

20 Points
□
□
50 Points
□
□
□
□
80 Points
□
□

Mercantilism

20-50-80 Menu

Objectives Covered Through This Menu and These Activities

- Students will discuss the political, economic, and social events and issues related to mercantilism.
- Students will create written, oral, and visual presentations of social studies information using effective communication skills, including proper citations and avoiding plagiarism.
- Students will use a variety of rich primary and secondary source material.
- Students will analyze information by applying absolute and relative chronology.
- Students will examine the impact of geographic factors on major events.

Materials Needed by Students for Completion

- Poster board or large white paper
- Blank index cards (for card sorts)
- Recording software or application (for videos)

Special Notes on the Use of This Menu

- This menu gives students the opportunity to create a video. The grading and sharing of these products can often be facilitated by having students prerecord their product using whatever technology is most convenient for the teacher. This allows the teacher to decide when it will be shown as well as keeps the presentation to its intended length. If recording options are limited, this activity can be modified by allowing students to act out the product (like a play) in front of the class.

Time Frame

- 1–2 weeks—Students are given a menu as the unit is started, and the teacher discusses all of the product options on the menu. As the different options are discussed, students will choose the activities they are most interested in completing so that they meet their goal of 100 points. As the lessons progress through the week(s), the teacher and students refer back to the menu options associated with the content being taught.

- 1–2 days—The teacher chooses an activity or product from the menu to use with the entire class.

Suggested Forms

- All-purpose rubric
- Proposal form for point-based projects
- Presentation rubric

Mercantilism

Directions: Choose at least two activities from the menu below. The activities must total 100 points. Place a checkmark next to each box to show which activities you will complete. All activities must be completed by _____ .

---

20 Points

❏ Create a folded quiz book to tests others' knowledge about mercantilism in the colonies.

❏ Assemble a card sort of actions that represent acceptable and unacceptable actions under the Navigation Acts.

---

50 Points

❏ Write and perform a speech in which you are a colonist expounding on the benefits of mercantilism.

❏ Draw a political cartoon that could have been published in England supporting the events occurring during this time.

❏ Prepare a poster that shares at least two primary and two secondary sources that demonstrate the political, cultural, and social aspects of the Navigation Acts.

❏ **Free choice on Mercantilism in the Colonies**—Prepare a proposal form and submit it to your teacher for approval.

---

80 Points

❏ Consider the political, economic, and social reasons for the Navigation Acts. Research laws or acts in the last century that were instated for similar reasons. Write an essay defending your findings.

❏ Develop a modern-day mercantilism system that could be implemented in your school. Record a video that explains the system from a political, economic, and social perspective.

Chapter 6

Building a New Nation

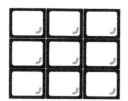

The American Revolution

Game Show Menu

Objectives Covered Through This Menu and These Activities

- Students will explain the roles played by significant individuals during the American Revolution.
- Students will discuss the political, economic, and social events and issues related to the American Revolution.
- Students will create written, oral, and visual presentations of social studies information using effective communication skills, including proper citations and avoiding plagiarism.
- Students will use a variety of rich primary and secondary source material.
- Students will apply the process of historical inquiry to research, interpret, and use multiple types of sources of evidence.
- Students will describe how the characteristics of and issues in U.S. history have been reflected in various genres of art, music, film, and literature.

Materials Needed by Students for Completion

- Poster board or large white paper
- Recording software or application (for commercials, videos)
- Blank index cards (for trading cards)
- Scrapbooking materials

Special Notes on the Use of This Menu

- This menu gives students the opportunity to create a video and commercial. The grading and sharing of these products can often be facilitated by having students prerecord their product using whatever technology is most convenient for the teacher. This allows the teacher to decide when it will be shown as well as keeps the presentation to its intended length. If recording options are limited, this activity can be modified by allowing students to act out the product (like a play) in front of the class.
- This menu provides the students the option of creating a visual presentation or product. This term has been included on the product guidelines, but it refers to students having a choice of what type of

visual product they would like to create. On the product guidelines, they will find a short list, but they are welcome to propose other web-based or tangible options.

Time Frame

- 2–3 weeks—Students are given their menu as the unit is started, and the guidelines and point expectations on the back of the menu are discussed. As lessons are taught throughout the unit, students and the teacher can refer back to the options associated with that topic (or column). The teacher will go over all of the options for the topic being covered and have students place checkmarks in the boxes next to the activities they are most interested in completing. As teaching continues over the next 2–3 weeks, activities are discussed, chosen, and submitted for grading.
- 1 week—At the beginning of the unit, the teacher chooses an activity from each area they feel would be most valuable for students. Stations can be set up in the classroom or one of the teacher-selected activities could be provided each day for completion. These activities are available for student choice throughout the week as regular instruction takes place.
- 1–2 days—The teacher chooses an activity from an objective to use with the entire class during that lesson time.

Suggested Forms

- All-purpose rubric
- Proposal form for point-based products
- Presentation rubric

Guidelines for the American Revolution Game Show Menu

- You must choose at least one activity from each topic area.
- You may not do more than two activities in any one topic area for credit. (You are, of course, welcome to do more than two for your own investigation.)
- Grading will be ongoing, so turn in products as you complete them.
- All free-choice proposals must be turned in and approved *prior* to working on the free choice.
- You must earn **150** points for a 100%. You may earn extra credit up to _____ points.
- You must show your teacher your plan for completion by: _____.

The American Revolution

	French and Indian War	Stamp and Townshend Acts	Coercive Acts	Declaration of Independence	Important Events	Historical Figures	Points for Each Level
	☐ Create a chart to show the political, economic, and social causes leading up to and following the French and Indian War. (15 pts.)	☐ Write Three Facts and a Fib that share the connection between the French Indian War and these taxation acts. (10 pts.)	☐ Draw a windowpane that states each of the Coercive Acts and their social impacts. (10 pts.)	☐ Create a mind map that shows the connections between ideas found in the Declaration of Independence. (15 pts.)	☐ Create a Venn diagram that compares the qualities of the colonies before and after the Revolutionary War. (10 pts.)	☐ Create a set of trading cards for the people who played major roles in the causes of the war. (15 pts.)	10–15 points
	☐ Locate primary and secondary sources associated with the French and Indian War. Use these sources to write a political newspaper article that may have been published in the colonies. (25 pts.)	☐ Record a commercial to support the Stamp or Townshend Acts that could have played in the colonies if they had that capability. (25 pts.)	☐ Design a pamphlet about these acts that could have been distributed when they were in effect. (20 pts.)	☐ Write an editorial for the newspaper that explains why a delegate might not want to sign the Declaration of Independence. (20 pts.)	☐ Design a Revolutionary War scrapbook that exemplifies why America won the Revolutionary War. (20 pts.)	☐ Pretend you are Haym Salomon and write a letter to your family about the importance of your role in the Revolutionary War. (20 pts.)	20–25 points
	☐ This war is considered a turning point in U.S. history. Record a video that traces its impact through history to the modern day. (30 pts.)	☐ Propose an alternative plan to either of these acts that could have changed the path of the American Revolution. (30 pts.)	☐ Prepare a product of your choice to show historical decisions in the past 2 centuries that were implemented for the same purposes as each act passed in 1774. (30 pts.)	☐ Consider a situation from which you would want to declare independence. Note your reasons and outline your own Declaration of Independence for the situation. (30 pts.)	☐ Some say the Battle of Saratoga was a turning point in history. Prepare a visual presentation to defend this point. (30 pts.)	☐ Come to school as Thomas Paine. Select a cause and speak out throughout the day against the cause as he would have. (30 pts.)	30 points
	Free Choice (prior approval) (10–30 pts.)	Free Choice (prior approval) (10–30 pts.)	Free Choice (prior approval) (10–30 pts.)	Free Choice (prior approval) (10–30 pts.)	Free Choice (prior approval) (10–30 pts.)	Free Choice (prior approval) (10–30 pts.)	10–30 points
	Total:	Total:	Total:	Total:	Total:	Total:	Total Grade:

Creating the Constitution

Meal Menu

Objectives Covered Through This Menu and These Activities

- Students will discuss the political, economic, and social events and issues related to the development of the Constitution.
- Students will evaluate the strengths and weaknesses of the Articles of Confederation and compare it to the U.S. Constitution.
- Students will evaluate the impact of Shays's Rebellion on the development of the Constitution.
- Students will use critical thinking skills and a variety of primary and secondary source material to explain and apply different methods that historians use to understand and interpret the past, including multiple points of view and historical context.
- Students will create visual representations of historical information.
- Students will analyze information by applying absolute and relative chronology.
- Students will examine the impact of geographic factors on major events.

Materials Needed by Students for Completion

- Poster board or large white paper
- Blank index cards (for card sorts)

Special Notes on the Use of This Menu

- This menu gives students the opportunity to create a video. The grading and sharing of these products can often be facilitated by having students prerecord their product using whatever technology is most convenient for the teacher. This allows the teacher to decide when it will be shown as well as keeps the presentation to its intended length. If recording options are limited, this activity can be modified by allowing students to act out the product (like a play) in front of the class.
- This menu gives students the opportunity to prepare a class demonstration. This can take a significant amount of time and organization. It can save time if the students who choose to do a demonstration can sign up for a designated day and time that is determined when the menu is distributed.

Time Frame

- 2–3 weeks—Students are given the menu as the unit is started. As the lesson or unit progresses throughout the week, students should refer to the menu options associated with that content. The teacher will go over all of the options for that objective and have students place a checkmark in the box for each option that represents the activity they are most interested in completing. As teaching continues, the activities chosen and completed should create a full day's meal, with a breakfast, a lunch, and a dinner. The teacher may choose to allow students time to work after other work is finished. When students complete the menu with this expectation, they have completed one activity from each content area, learning style, or level of Bloom's revised taxonomy, depending on the design of the menu.
- 1 week—At the start of the unit, the teacher chooses one activity from each meal family they feel are most valuable for students. Stations can be set up in the classroom. These three activities are available for student choice throughout the week as regular instruction takes place.
- 1–2 days—The teacher chooses an activity or product from an objective to use with the entire class during that lesson time. Additionally, the teacher could choose one of the two desserts as an enrichment activity.

Suggested Forms

- All-purpose rubric
- Free-choice proposal form
- Presentation rubric

Creating the Constitution

Directions: Choose one activity each for breakfast, lunch, and dinner. Dessert is an activity you can choose to do after you have finished your other meals. All products must be completed by: _____ .

Breakfast

- ☐ Make a T-chart that shares the strengths and weaknesses of the Articles of Confederation.
- ☐ Create a quiz to test your classmates on the supports for the Articles of Confederation and the impacts of their weaknesses.
- ☐ Design an advertisement that could be used to explain the impacts of the Northwest Ordinance of 1787 on colonists based on where they lived.

Lunch

- ☐ Prepare a class demonstration that allows your classmates to experience the political and economic causes that led to Shays's Rebellion.
- ☐ Music can give meaning to historical events. Record an original song that tells about Shays's Rebellion and its impact on the development of the Constitution.
- ☐ Draw a map of the different landmarks related to Shays's Rebellion on a poster. Include how each landmark impacted the progress of Shays's Rebellion.

Dinner

- ☐ Present a Venn diagram to compare the organization of the federal government before and after the ratification of the Constitution.
- ☐ Assemble a card sort of provisions that were included in the Constitution submitted to the states in 1787 and those that were not.
- ☐ Locate at least two primary and secondary Anti-Federalist sources from the Great Debate. Based on these sources, record your own Anti-Federalist speech to share your concerns about the Constitution.

Dessert

- ☐ Although written many years ago, the Constitution still has impact on Americans of all ages. Design an informational video on the Constitution and its importance to people your age.
- ☐ Create a social media profile for Alexander Hamilton during the Constitutional Convention. His profile should include not only posts and interactions with other delegates, but also some live videos of the experience!
- ☐ **Free choice on the impact of the Constitution**—Prepare a proposal form and submit it to your teacher for approval.

Building a New Nation

Game Show Menu

Objectives Covered Through This Menu and These Activities

- Students will analyze Alexander Hamilton's policies and proposals and George Washington's Farewell Address.
- Students will investigate Thomas Jefferson's and James Monroe's national impacts during their presidencies as well as historical events that followed.
- Students will examine the Marshall Court's and the War of 1812's impact on the building of our nation.
- Students will discuss the political, economic, and social events and issues related to the national events from 1789–1812.
- Students will create written, oral, and visual presentations of social studies information using effective communication skills, including proper citations and avoiding plagiarism.
- Students will create visual representations of historical information.
- Students will use a variety of rich primary and secondary source material.
- Students will apply the process of historical inquiry to research, interpret, and use multiple types of sources of evidence.
- Students will describe how the characteristics of and issues in U.S. history have been reflected in literature.

Materials Needed by Students for Completion

- Poster board or large white paper
- Graph paper or Internet access (for WebQuests)
- Recording software or application (for videos)
- Blank index cards (for card sorts)

Special Notes on the Use of This Menu

- This menu gives students the opportunity to create a video. The grading and sharing of these products can often be facilitated by having students prerecord their product using whatever technology is most convenient for the teacher. This allows the teacher to decide when it will be shown as well as keeps the presentation to its intended length.

If recording options are limited, this activity can be modified by allowing students to act out the product (like a play) in front of the class.

- This menu gives students the opportunity to facilitate a class model. The expectation is that all students in the classroom will play an active role in the model. This may mean that students need some additional space for their model.

- This menu allows students to create a WebQuest. There are multiple versions and templates for WebQuests available on the Internet. It is your decision whether you would like to specify a format or if you will allow students to create one of their own choosing.

- This menu provides the students the option of creating a visual presentation or product. This term has been included on the product guidelines, but it refers to students having a choice of what type of visual product they would like to create. On the product guidelines, they will find a short list, but they are welcome to propose other web-based or tangible options.

Time Frame

- 2–3 weeks—Students are given their menu as the unit is started, and the guidelines and point expectations on the back of the menu are discussed. As lessons are taught throughout the unit, students and the teacher can refer back to the options associated with that topic (or column). The teacher will go over all of the options for the topic being covered and have students place checkmarks in the boxes next to the activities they are most interested in completing. As teaching continues over the next 2–3 weeks, activities are discussed, chosen, and submitted for grading.

- 1 week—At the beginning of the unit, the teacher chooses an activity from each area they feel would be most valuable for students. Stations can be set up in the classroom or one of the teacher-selected activities could be provided each day for completion. These activities are available for student choice throughout the week as regular instruction takes place.

- 1–2 days—The teacher chooses an activity from an objective to use with the entire class during that lesson time.

Suggested Forms

- All-purpose rubric
- Proposal form for point-based products
- Presentation rubric

Guidelines for the Building a New Nation Game Show Menu

- You must choose at least one activity from each topic area.
- You may not do more than two activities in any one topic area for credit. (You are, of course, welcome to do more than two for your own investigation.)
- Grading will be ongoing, so turn in products as you complete them.
- All free-choice proposals must be turned in and approved prior to working on the free choice.
- You must earn **150** points for a 100%. You may earn extra credit up to _____ points.
- You must show your teacher your plan for completion by: _____.

Building a New Nation

Alexander Hamilton	National Unity	Thomas Jefferson	The Marshall Court	The War of 1812	James Monroe	Points for Each Level
☐ Write a folded quiz book about Hamilton's policies and proposals. (15 pts.)	☐ Design a cartoon to portray George Washington's Farewell Address and its impact on foreign policy under James Adams. (15 pts.)	☐ Compose Three Facts and a Fib about the "Revolution of 1800." (15 pts.)	☐ Draw a windowpane to show the beliefs of the Marshall Court. Include a court case to support each belief. (10 pts.)	☐ Create a card sort to determine the political and economic causes and consequences of the War of 1812. (15 pts.)	☐ Create a poster or visual to represent different events and their social impacts during the Era of Good Feelings. (15 pts.)	10–15 points
☐ Consider each of Hamilton's policies. Prepare a document that shows the social and political impacts of his policies in the 1700s and today. (25 pts.)	☐ Create a classroom model that demonstrates the political and economic impacts of Washington's Farewell Address on future historical events. (25 pts.)	☐ Write a letter that Jefferson may have written to a political friend detailing the social and economic impacts he hopes to have on the states. (25 pts.)	☐ Write three journal entries that share John Marshall's views on various Supreme Court cases. (25 pts.)	☐ Research the casualties of the War of 1812. Prepare an obituary for an impressed sailor. (20 pts.)	☐ Record a video defending the claim that the Missouri Compromise was a turning point in history. (25 pts.)	20–25 points
☐ Assemble a WebQuest that helps questors experience Hamilton's encounters with supporters and debaters through his eyes. (30 pts.)	☐ Record a video in which you portray Washington discussing the nation and his view on its policies today. (30 pts.)	☐ Prepare a student-taught lesson about the impact of the Louisiana Purchase on at least two other historical events. (30 pts.)	☐ Using all of the members of your class, create an original case to be tried in the Marshall Court. (30 pts.)	☐ Read the poem "Old Ironsides" by Oliver Wendell Holmes. Prepare a visual presentation that analyzes the meaning of the stanzas and indicates the importance of this written work in history. (30 pts.)	☐ Monroe's time in office was a turning point in U.S. history. Prepare a speech that supports or denies this claim. Use primary and secondary sources as evidentiary support when possible. (30 pts.)	30 points
Free Choice (prior approval) (10–30 pts.)	Free Choice (prior approval) (10–30 pts.)	Free Choice (prior approval) (10–30 pts.)	Free Choice (prior approval) (10–30 pts.)	Free Choice (prior approval) (10–30 pts.)	Free Choice (prior approval) (10–30 pts.)	10–30 points
Total:	Total:	Total:	Total:	Total:	Total:	Total Grade:

Name:_____ Date:_____

```
┌─────────────┐
│ 20 Points   │
│ ▢ _____   │
│ ▢ _____   │
│ 50 Points   │
│ ▢ _____   │
│ ▢ _____   │
│ ▢ _____   │
│ ▢ _____   │
│ 80 Points   │
│ ▢ _____   │
│ ▢ _____   │
└─────────────┘
```

Native Americans and Jackson

20-50-80 Menu

Objectives Covered Through This Menu and These Activities

- Students will examine the events and decisions related to the resettlement and removal of the Cherokee Indians during the Jacksonian era.
- Students will create written, oral, and visual presentations of social studies information using effective communication skills, including proper citations and avoiding plagiarism.
- Students will create visual representations of historical information.
- Students will use critical thinking skills and a variety of primary source material to explain and apply different methods that historians use to understand and interpret the past, including multiple points of view and historical context.
- Students will apply the process of historical inquiry to research, interpret, and use multiple types of sources of evidence.
- Students will examine the impact of supreme court cases on historical events.

Materials Needed by Students for Completion

- Poster board or large white paper
- Magazines (for collages)
- Recording software or application (for documentary)

Special Notes on the Use of This Menu

- This menu gives students the opportunity to create a documentary. The grading and sharing of these products can often be facilitated by having students prerecord their product using whatever technology is most convenient for the teacher. This allows the teacher to decide when it will be shown as well as keeps the presentation to its intended length. If recording options are limited, this activity can be modified by allowing students to act out the product (like a play) in front of the class.
- This menu provides the students the option of creating a visual presentation or product. This term has been included on the product guidelines, but it refers to students having a choice of what type of visual product they would like to create. On the product guidelines,

they will find a short list, but they are welcome to propose other web-based or tangible options.

Time Frame

- 1–2 weeks—Students are given a menu as the unit is started, and the teacher discusses all of the product options on the menu. As the different options are discussed, students will choose the activities they are most interested in completing so that they meet their goal of 100 points. As the lessons progress through the week(s), the teacher and students refer back to the menu options associated with the content being taught.
- 1–2 days—The teacher chooses an activity or product from the menu to use with the entire class.

Suggested Forms

- All-purpose rubric
- Proposal form for point-based projects
- Presentation rubric

Name:_____ Date:_____

Native Americans and Jackson

Directions: Choose at least two activities from the menu below. The activities must total 100 points. Place a checkmark next to each box to show which activities you will complete. All activities must be completed by _____ .

---

20 Points

❏ Design a brochure about the events and decisions related to the resettlement and removal of the Cherokee Indians during the Jacksonian era.

❏ Assemble a collage of pictures and words that represent different aspects of the Indian resettlement process. Label each item with the events it represents.

---

50 Points

❏ Write a newspaper article that documents the events leading up and following the implementation of Andrew Jackson's Native American Policy.

❏ Create a poster or visual presentation to represent the social impacts of Jackson's decision to not recognize *Worcester v. Georgia*.

❏ Write three journals entries from the perspective of a Cherokee before, during, and after *Worcester v. Georgia*.

❏ **Free choice on Jackson's Impact on Native Americans**—Prepare a proposal form and submit it to your teacher for approval.

---

80 Points

❏ You have been asked to provide a basis for Jackson's decision to refuse to recognize *Worcester v. Georgia*. Write an analysis essay that supports his decision. Include at least two primary sources as evidentiary support.

❏ Consider the impact of *Worcester v. Georgia* being recognized on upcoming historical events. Record a what-if documentary in which you share how the following 100 years may have been different if Jackson had recognized this ruling.

Antebellum America

Game Show Menu

Objectives Covered Through This Menu and These Activities

- Students will determine the societal impacts of the Second Great Awakening.
- Students will examine the role of women, reformists, and abolitionists in Antebellum America.
- Students will discuss the political, economic, and social events and issues related to Antebellum America.
- Students will create written, oral, and visual presentations of social studies information using effective communication skills, including proper citations and avoiding plagiarism.
- Students will use a variety of rich primary and secondary source material.
- Students will analyze information by applying absolute and relative chronology.
- Students will use social studies terminology correctly.
- Students will describe how the characteristics of and issues in U.S. history have been reflected in various genres of art.

Materials Needed by Students for Completion

- Poster board or large white paper
- Materials for bulletin board display
- Magazines (for collages)
- Large blank lined index cards (for instruction cards)
- Recording software or application (for videos)
- Blank index cards (for trading cards)

Special Notes on the Use of This Menu

- This menu gives students the opportunity to create a video. The grading and sharing of these products can often be facilitated by having students prerecord their product using whatever technology is most convenient for the teacher. This allows the teacher to decide when it will be shown as well as keeps the presentation to its intended length. If recording options are limited, this activity can be modified by allowing students to act out the product (like a play) in front of the class.

- This menu gives students the opportunity to teach a concept. This can take a significant amount of time and organization. It can save time if the students who choose to do a lesson can sign up for a designated day and time that is determined when the menu is distributed.
- This menu allows students to create a bulletin board display. Some classrooms may only have one bulletin board, so the teacher can divide the board into sections, or additional classroom wall or hall space can be sectioned off for the creation of these displays. Students can plan their display based on the amount of space they are assigned.

Time Frame

- 2–3 weeks—Students are given their menu as the unit is started, and the guidelines and point expectations on the back of the menu are discussed. As lessons are taught throughout the unit, students and the teacher can refer back to the options associated with that topic (or column). The teacher will go over all of the options for the topic being covered and have students place checkmarks in the boxes next to the activities they are most interested in completing. As teaching continues over the next 2–3 weeks, activities are discussed, chosen, and submitted for grading.
- 1 week—At the beginning of the unit, the teacher chooses an activity from each area they feel would be most valuable for students. Stations can be set up in the classroom or one of the teacher-selected activities could be provided each day for completion. These activities are available for student choice throughout the week as regular instruction takes place.
- 1–2 days—The teacher chooses an activity from an objective to use with the entire class during that lesson time.

Suggested Forms

- All-purpose rubric
- Student-taught lesson rubric
- Proposal form for point-based products
- Presentation rubric

Guidelines for the Antebellum America Game Show Menu

- You must choose at least one activity from each topic area.
- You may not do more than two activities in any one topic area for credit. (You are, of course, welcome to do more than two for your own investigation.)
- Grading will be ongoing, so turn in products as you complete them.
- All free-choice proposals must be turned in and approved *prior* to working on the free choice.
- You must earn **130** points for a 100%. You may earn extra credit up to _____ points.
- You must show your teacher your plan for completion by: _____.

Name:_____ Date:_____

Antebellum America

The Second Great Awakening	Abolition and Abolitionists	Reform Movements	Roles of Women	Historic Figures	Points for Each Level
☐ Write Three Facts and a Fib about societal and political impacts of the Second Great Awakening. (15 pts.)	☐ Create a collage of quotes from William Lloyd Garrison's *The Liberator*. Include a brief social and political analysis for each quote. (15 pts.)	☐ Prepare a poster or visual to show the obvious and subtle connections between the different reform movements in this time period. (15 pts.)	☐ Write an instruction card that details the different societal roles of women during this time. (10 pts.)	☐ Create a set of trading cards for the historical figures found in this time period. (10 pts.)	10–15 points
☐ Build a bulletin board display to share the causes and cultural impacts of the Second Great Awakening. (20 pts.)	☐ Write a newspaper article describing the work and political impact of the American Colonization Society. (25 pts.)	☐ Write interview questions for one of the reformers about their political impacts. Using primary sources to understand their voice, create responses that would represent their view. (25 pts.)	☐ Record a video that supports the ideals of the cult of domesticity. Include its social, cultural, and economic benefits. (25 pts.)	☐ Develop a social media profile for Elizabeth Cady Stanton, Lucretia Mott, or Dorothea Dix. (25 pts.)	20–25 points
☐ After researching how the Second Great Awakening impacted art, create your own original piece of art to represent the Second Great Awakening. (30 pts.)	☐ Record an original speech that Frederick Douglass may have given to champion equal rights. Use primary and secondary sources to include some of Douglass's words in this speech. (30 pts.)	☐ Which reformer had the largest impact on our culture today? Select a reformer and design a product of your choice to defend your choice. (30 pts.)	☐ The Seneca Falls Convention is considered the impetus for modern-day feminism. Brainstorm a student-taught lesson to investigate this connection. (30 pts.)	☐ Invent a class game to help your classmates process the works and impacts of historical figures during this time period. (30 pts.)	30 points
Free Choice (prior approval) (10–30 pts.)	**Free Choice** (prior approval) (10–30 pts.)	**Free Choice** (prior approval) (10–30 pts.)	**Free Choice** (prior approval) (10–30 pts.)	**Free Choice** (prior approval) (10–30 pts.)	10–30 points
Total:	**Total:**	**Total:**	**Total:**	**Total:**	**Total Grade:**

CHAPTER 7

Road to the Civil War

Territorial Expansion

Tic-Tac-Toe Menu

Objectives Covered Through This Menu and These Activities
- Students will discuss the political, economic, and social events and issues related to Manifest Destiny, the Mexican-American War, and the Wilmot Proviso.
- Students will create visual representations of historical information.
- Students will use a variety of rich primary and secondary source material.
- Students will analyze information by applying absolute and relative chronology.
- Students will describe how the characteristics of and issues in U.S. history have been reflected in various genres of art.

Materials Needed by Students for Completion
- Poster board or large white paper
- Graph paper or Internet access (for WebQuests)
- Blank index cards (for card sorts)
- Magazines (for collages)
- Recording software or application (for videos)

Special Notes on the Use of This Menu
- This menu gives students the opportunity to create a video. The grading and sharing of these products can often be facilitated by having students prerecord their product using whatever technology is most convenient for the teacher. This allows the teacher to decide when it will be shown as well as keeps the presentation to its intended length. If recording options are limited, this activity can be modified by allowing students to act out the product (like a play) in front of the class.
- This menu allows students to create a WebQuest. There are multiple versions and templates for WebQuests available on the Internet. It is your decision whether you would like to specify a format or if you will allow students to create one of their own choosing.

Time Frame

- 2–3 weeks—Students are given the menu as the unit is started. The teacher will go over all of the options for that content and have students place checkmarks in the boxes that represent the activities they are most interested in completing. As students choose activities, they should complete a column or a row. When students complete this pattern, they have completed one activity from each content area, learning style, or level of Bloom's revised taxonomy, depending on the design of the menu. As the teacher presents lessons throughout the week, they should refer back to the menu options associated with that content.
- 1 week—At the start of the unit, the teacher chooses the three activities they feel are most valuable for students. Stations can be set up in the classroom. These three activities are available for student choice throughout the week as regular instruction takes place.
- 1–2 days—The teacher chooses an activity from the menu to use with the entire class.

Suggested Forms

- All-purpose rubric
- Free-choice proposal form
- Presentation rubric

Territorial Expansion

Directions: Check the boxes you plan to complete. They should form a tic-tac-toe across or down. All products are due by: _____ .

☐ *Manifest Destiny* Research John L. O'Sullivan's famous words about Manifest Destiny. Evaluate his statement and create a WebQuest to show the consequences of his words.	☐ *The Mexican-American War* Prepare a card sort to help others determine supporters and opposers of the Mexican-American War as well as understand reasons for their views. Include quotes from primary sources when possible.	☐ *The Wilmot Proviso* The Wilmot Proviso was never ratified. Write three journal entries Wilmot may have written: one when he proposed his Proviso, one when it was presented to the Senate, and one as he reflected on its consequences.
☐ *The Wilmot Proviso* Design a social media profile for David Wilmot in which he shares his hopes for the impacts and ultimately the consequences of his proviso. Be creative!	☐ **Free Choice:** **Manifest Destiny** (Fill out your proposal form before beginning the free choice!)	☐ *The Mexican-American War* Create a collage of different works of art that represented societal perceptions of the Mexican-American War. Include a description of the work and its representation of perceptions.
☐ *The Mexican-American War* The Mexican-American War is considered a turning point in history. Create a political cartoon that illustrates its contributions to sectionalism.	☐ *The Wilmot Proviso* Record a video to analyze how the political environment in the House and Senate impacted the passing of the Proviso. Hypothesize possible steps for the Senate to pass the Proviso and the subsequent changes to the known consequences.	☐ *Manifest Destiny* Although acquiring territories often has political motivations, write a newspaper article explaining the social and economic motivations behind the acquisition of Texas and Oregon.

Road to the Civil War

Tic-Tac-Toe Menu

Objectives Covered Through This Menu and These Activities

- Students will discuss the political, economic, and social events and issues related to the various actions that lead up to the Civil War, including the Compromise of 1850, the Fugitive Slave Act, *Uncle Tom's Cabin*, the Kansas-Nebraska Act, the Dred Scott case, and Harpers Ferry.
- Students will create visual representations of historical information.
- Students will use a variety of rich primary and secondary source material.
- Students will analyze information by applying absolute and relative chronology.
- Students will identify bias and support with historical evidence.
- Students will apply the process of historical inquiry to research, interpret, and use multiple types of sources of evidence.
- Students will describe how the characteristics of and issues in U.S. history have been reflected in various genres of music.

Materials Needed by Students for Completion

- Poster board or large white paper
- Materials for three-dimensional timelines
- Recording software or application (for videos)

Special Notes on the Use of This Menu

- This menu gives students the opportunity to create a video. The grading and sharing of these products can often be facilitated by having students prerecord their product using whatever technology is most convenient for the teacher. This allows the teacher to decide when it will be shown as well as keeps the presentation to its intended length. If recording options are limited, this activity can be modified by allowing students to act out the product (like a play) in front of the class.
- This menu gives students the opportunity to facilitate a class model. The expectation is that all students in the classroom will play an active role in the model. This may mean that students need some additional space for their model.

- This menu provides the students the option of creating a visual presentation or product. This term has been included on the product guidelines, but it refers to students having a choice of what type of visual product they would like to create. On the product guidelines, they will find a short list, but they are welcome to propose other web-based or tangible options.

Time Frame

- 2–3 weeks—Students are given the menu as the unit is started. The teacher will go over all of the options for that content and have students place checkmarks in the boxes that represent the activities they are most interested in completing. As students choose activities, they should complete a column or a row. When students complete this pattern, they have completed one activity from each content area, learning style, or level of Bloom's revised taxonomy, depending on the design of the menu. As the teacher presents lessons throughout the week, they should refer back to the menu options associated with that content.
- 1 week—At the start of the unit, the teacher chooses the three activities they feel are most valuable for students. Stations can be set up in the classroom. These three activities are available for student choice throughout the week as regular instruction takes place.
- 1–2 days—The teacher chooses an activity from the menu to use with the entire class.

Suggested Forms

- All-purpose rubric
- Free-choice proposal form
- Presentation rubric

Name:_____ Date:_____

Road to the Civil War

Directions: Check the boxes you plan to complete. They should form a tic-tac-toe across or down. All products are due by: _____ .

☐ *Compromise of 1850* Henry Clay considered different proposals before suggesting the Compromise of 1850. Draw a mind map to break down the proposals and their impacts on the North and South.	☐ *Kansas-Nebraska Act* Record a video in which you detail the causes and social and political consequences of the Kansas-Nebraska Act. Hypothesize the impacts of someone other than Stephen A. Douglas introducing the act.	☐ *Fugitive Slave Act* Create a three-dimensional timeline to show how the Fugitive Slave Act fit into and affected the social and political events of the 1850s.
☐ *Dred Scott Case* Create a quiz about the Dred Scott case, including its connection to the Missouri Compromise and, ultimately, the 13th Amendment.	☐ **Free Choice: Event During the 1850s That Contributed to the Civil War** (Fill out your proposal form before beginning the free choice!)	☐ *Uncle Tom's Cabin* Analyze primary and secondary source book reviews written about *Uncle Tom's Cabin* by Northerners and Southerners. Prepare a visual presentation that shares your findings.
☐ *Harpers Ferry* Listen to the song "John Brown's Body." Evaluate the accuracy of the information provided in the song, and create a visual presentation to share the song and your evaluation.	☐ *Lincoln-Douglas Debates* Prepare a class model in which your classmates get to participate in an activity that allows them to experience the Lincoln-Douglas debates.	☐ *The Crittenden Compromise* Write a letter that Crittenden could have written to Lincoln to accompany his proposal and persuade Lincoln to accept his compromise.

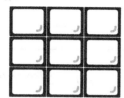

The Civil War

Game Show Menu

Objectives Covered Through This Menu and These Activities

- Students will discuss the political, economic, and social events and issues related to the secession process, the Emancipation Proclamation, and the Republican congress.
- Students will create written, oral, and visual presentations of social studies information using effective communication skills, including proper citations and avoiding plagiarism.
- Students will use a variety of rich primary and secondary source material.
- Students will analyze information by applying absolute and relative chronology.
- Students will identify bias and support with historical evidence.
- Students will describe how the characteristics of and issues in U.S. history have been reflected in various genres of art and music.

Materials Needed by Students for Completion

- Poster board or large white paper
- Recording software or application (for videos)
- Recycled materials (for models)
- Magazines (for collages)
- Graph paper or Internet access (for WebQuests)
- Blank index cards (for card sorts)

Special Notes on the Use of This Menu

- This menu gives students the opportunity to create a video. The grading and sharing of these products can often be facilitated by having students prerecord their product using whatever technology is most convenient for the teacher. This allows the teacher to decide when it will be shown as well as keeps the presentation to its intended length. If recording options are limited, this activity can be modified by allowing students to act out the product (like a play) in front of the class.
- This menu asks students to use recycled materials to create their model. This does not mean only plastic and paper; instead, students should focus on using materials in new ways. It works well if a box

is started for "recycled" contributions at the beginning of the school year. That way, students always have access to these types of materials.

- This menu gives students the opportunity to facilitate a class game. The expectation is that all students in the classroom will play an active role in the game. This may mean that the facilitator may need some additional space and time for their game. This can take a significant amount of time and organization. It can save time if all of the students who choose to present their game can sign up for a designated day and time that is determined when the menu is distributed.

- This menu gives students the opportunity to teach a concept. This can take a significant amount of time and organization. It can save time if the students who choose to do a lesson can sign up for a designated day and time that is determined when the menu is distributed.

- This menu allows students to create a WebQuest. There are multiple versions and templates for WebQuests available on the Internet. It is your decision whether you would like to specify a format or if you will allow students to create one of their own choosing.

- This menu provides the students the option of creating a visual presentation or product. This term has been included on the product guidelines, but it refers to students having a choice of what type of visual product they would like to create. On the product guidelines, they will find a short list, but they are welcome to propose other web-based or tangible options.

Time Frame

- 2–3 weeks—Students are given their menu as the unit is started, and the guidelines and point expectations on the back of the menu are discussed. As lessons are taught throughout the unit, students and the teacher can refer back to the options associated with that topic (or column). The teacher will go over all of the options for the topic being covered and have students place checkmarks in the boxes next to the activities they are most interested in completing. As teaching continues over the next 2–3 weeks, activities are discussed, chosen, and submitted for grading.

- 1 week—At the beginning of the unit, the teacher chooses an activity from each area they feel would be most valuable for students. Stations can be set up in the classroom or one of the teacher-selected activities could be provided each day for completion. These activities are available for student choice throughout the week as regular instruction takes place.

- 1–2 days—The teacher chooses an activity from an objective to use with the entire class during that lesson time.

Suggested Forms

- All-purpose rubric
- Student-taught lesson rubric
- Proposal form for point-based products
- Presentation rubric

Guidelines for the Civil War Game Show Menu

- You must choose at least one activity from each topic area.
- You may not do more than two activities in any one topic area for credit. (You are, of course, welcome to do more than two for your own investigation.)
- Grading will be ongoing, so turn in products as you complete them.
- All free-choice proposals must be turned in and approved *prior* to working on the free choice.
- You must earn **130** points for a 100%. You may earn extra credit up to _____ points.
- You must show your teacher your plan for completion by: _____.

Name:_____ Date:_____

The Civil War

Secession	The North	The South	The Republican Congress	Emancipation Proclamation	Consequences of the War	Points for Each Level
☐ Create a brochure that compares the components of the U.S. Constitution and the Confederate Constitution. (15 pts.)	☐ Build a model that exemplifies the advantages and disadvantages of the North. (10 pts.)	☐ Assemble a collage that represents the benefits of fighting a defensive war. Include a Civil War example with each item. (10 pts.)	☐ Make a foldable to discuss the different Acts implemented by the Republican congress. Include how each affected the North and the South. (10 pts.)	☐ Draw a windowpane that shows the important aspects of this document and the political impacts of each. (10 pts.)	☐ Create a card sort in which users sort different consequences of the Civil War for the North, South, women, federal government, and freed slaves. (10 pts.)	10–15 points
☐ Evaluate the claim that Fort Sumter caused the Civil War. Write an essay in which you address this claim from multiple perspectives. (25 pts.)	☐ Write a newspaper article that extenuates the most significant disadvantage of the North. (25 pts.)	☐ Draw a Venn diagram to show the relationship between states' rights and a central government as they affected the war in the South. (20 pts.)	☐ Propose a class game to help others process reasons for and influences of the various Acts passed in 1862–1883. (25 pts.)	☐ Prepare a WebQuest that allows questors to experience the impact of this document on the Union Army as well as contrabands of war. (25 pts.)	☐ Choose a Civil War movie. Analyze its historical accuracy as it relates to the known consequences of the war. Make a product of your choice to share your analyses. (25 pts.)	20–25 points
☐ Research Lincoln's impact on the South's secession. Do you think he could have done or said something that would have led to another outcome? Record a video to share your thoughts. (30 pts.)	☐ Locate at least four primary and/or secondary sources detailing the advantages of the North during the Civil War. Prepare a visual presentation in which you share potential bias in each. (30 pts.)	☐ Research the Southern songs or art from the Civil War and record a video in which you perform one of the songs or analyze a work of art and discuss its connection with the Civil War. (30 pts.)	☐ Consider all of the Acts passed in 1862 and 1863. Which would have the greatest impact on reconstruction efforts? Write an essay to explain and support your choice. (30 pts.)	☐ Record a video or design a webpage or blog that shares the alignment between this document and the work of Dr. Martin Luther King, Jr. (30 pts.)	☐ Create a student-taught lesson to facilitate understanding the social and political consequences of the Civil War on the different groups of people. (30 pts.)	30 points
Free Choice (prior approval) (10–30 pts.)	**Free Choice** (prior approval) (10–30 pts.)	**Free Choice** (prior approval) (10–30 pts.)	**Free Choice** (prior approval) (10–30 pts.)	**Free Choice** (prior approval) (10–30 pts.)	**Free Choice** (prior approval) (10–30 pts.)	10–30 points
Total:	Total:	Total:	Total:	Total:	Total:	Total Grade:

Reconstruction Amendments

Tic-Tac-Toe Menu

Objectives Covered Through This Menu and These Activities

- Students will discuss the political, economic, and social events and issues related to the 13th, 14th, and 15th Amendments to the Constitution.
- Students will create written, oral, and visual presentations of social studies information using effective communication skills, including proper citations and avoiding plagiarism.
- Students will analyze information by applying absolute and relative chronology.
- Students will use social studies terminology correctly.

Materials Needed by Students for Completion

- Poster board or large white paper
- Large blank lined index cards (for instruction cards)
- Blank index cards (for card sorts)
- Recording software or application (for videos)

Special Notes on the Use of This Menu

- This menu gives students the opportunity to create a video. The grading and sharing of these products can often be facilitated by having students prerecord their product using whatever technology is most convenient for the teacher. This allows the teacher to decide when it will be shown as well as keeps the presentation to its intended length. If recording options are limited, this activity can be modified by allowing students to act out the product (like a play) in front of the class.
- This menu gives students the opportunity to teach a concept. This can take a significant amount of time and organization. It can save time if the students who choose to do a lesson can sign up for a designated day and time that is determined when the menu is distributed.
- This menu provides the students the option of creating a visual presentation or product. This term has been included on the product guidelines, but it refers to students having a choice of what type of visual product they would like to create. On the product guidelines,

they will find a short list, but they are welcome to propose other web-based or tangible options.

Time Frame

- 2–3 weeks—Students are given the menu as the unit is started. The teacher will go over all of the options for that content and have students place checkmarks in the boxes that represent the activities they are most interested in completing. As students choose activities, they should complete a column or a row. When students complete this pattern, they have completed one activity from each content area, learning style, or level of Bloom's revised taxonomy, depending on the design of the menu. As the teacher presents lessons throughout the week, they should refer back to the menu options associated with that content.
- 1 week—At the start of the unit, the teacher chooses the three activities they feel are most valuable for students. Stations can be set up in the classroom. These three activities are available for student choice throughout the week as regular instruction takes place.
- 1–2 days—The teacher chooses an activity from the menu to use with the entire class.

Suggested Forms

- All-purpose rubric
- Free-choice proposal form
- Presentation rubric
- Student-taught lesson rubric

Reconstruction Amendments

Directions: Check the boxes you plan to complete. They should form a tic-tac-toe across or down. All products are due by: _____ .

☐ *13th Amendment* Lincoln had to strategize to get this amendment passed. Write an instruction card that could be used to show the process he followed in 1864–1865.	☐ *14th Amendment* Draw a T-chart to organize the pros and cons of this amendment as it was viewed from various states.	☐ *15th Amendment* Write and record a speech that a suffragette may have given regarding the 15th Amendment and its impact on women's rights.
☐ *15th Amendment* Write an essay about the intentions of the 15th Amendment and how different stakeholders reacted to the amendment.	☐ **Free Choice: 13th Amendment** (Fill out your proposal form before beginning the free choice!)	☐ *14th Amendment* Congress required the ratification of this amendment in order to participate in certain governmental processes. Assemble a card sort to determine what states could/could not do depending on their stance on this amendment.
☐ *14th Amendment* After reading all of the sections of this amendment, which section has had the greatest impact on the Civil Rights Movement? Record a video discussing the sections of the amendment and defending your choice.	☐ *15th Amendment* Prepare a student-created lesson to teach others about the interconnectedness of the Reconstruction Amendments as well as their impact on modern-day politics.	☐ *13th Amendment* Select a political cartoon (that you have not already discussed) that represents this amendment. Create a visual presentation that analyzes the selected cartoon.

CHAPTER 8

Growth of the United States

The West

Meal Menu

Objectives Covered Through This Menu and These Activities

- Students will discuss the political, economic, and social events and issues related to the Transcontinental Railroad and diversity in the West.
- Students will create visual representations of historical information.
- Students will use a variety of rich primary and secondary source material.
- Students will apply the process of historical inquiry to research, interpret, and use multiple types of sources of evidence.
- Students will describe how the characteristics of and issues in U.S. history have been reflected in various genres of art, music, film, and literature.
- Students will analyze the impact of technological innovations on American life.

Materials Needed by Students for Completion

- Poster board or large white paper
- Blank index cards (for trading cards)
- Graph paper or Internet access (for crossword puzzles, WebQuests)
- Scrapbooking materials (or electronic portfolios)
- Recording software or application (for documentaries)

Special Notes on the Use of This Menu

- This menu gives students the opportunity to create a documentary. The grading and sharing of these products can often be facilitated by having students prerecord their product using whatever technology is most convenient for the teacher. This allows the teacher to decide when it will be shown as well as keeps the presentation to its intended length. If recording options are limited, this activity can be modified by allowing students to act out the product (like a play) in front of the class.
- This menu gives students the opportunity to teach a concept. This can take a significant amount of time and organization. It can save

time if the students who choose to do a lesson can sign up for a designated day and time that is determined when the menu is distributed.

- This menu allows students to create a WebQuest. There are multiple versions and templates for WebQuests available on the Internet. It is your decision whether you would like to specify a format or if you will allow students to create one of their own choosing.
- This menu provides the students the option of creating a visual presentation or product. This term has been included on the product guidelines, but it refers to students having a choice of what type of visual product they would like to create. On the product guidelines, they will find a short list, but they are welcome to propose other web-based or tangible options.

Time Frame

- 2–3 weeks—Students are given the menu as the unit is started. As the lesson or unit progresses throughout the week, students should refer to the menu options associated with that content. The teacher will go over all of the options for that objective and have students place a checkmark in the box for each option that represents the activity they are most interested in completing. As teaching continues, the activities chosen and completed should create a full day's meal, with a breakfast, a lunch, and a dinner. The teacher may choose to allow students time to work after other work is finished. When students complete the menu with this expectation, they have completed one activity from each content area, learning style, or level of Bloom's revised taxonomy, depending on the design of the menu.
- 1 week—At the start of the unit, the teacher chooses one activity from each meal family they feel are most valuable for students. Stations can be set up in the classroom. These three activities are available for student choice throughout the week as regular instruction takes place.
- 1–2 days—The teacher chooses an activity or product from an objective to use with the entire class during that lesson time. Additionally, the teacher could choose one of the two desserts as an enrichment activity.

Suggested Forms

- All-purpose rubric
- Free-choice proposal form
- Presentation rubric
- Student-taught lesson rubric

Name:_____ Date:_____

The West

Directions: Choose one activity each for breakfast, lunch, and dinner. Dessert is an activity you can choose to do after you have finished your other meals. All products must be completed by: _____ .

Breakfast
- ☐ Assemble a set of trading cards that includes the diverse groups who lived and/or migrated to the West in the late 1800s.
- ☐ Draw a triple Venn diagram to compare the lives and drives of three different groups who lived in the West during this time.
- ☐ Design a WebQuest that introduces users to the art, music, and literature associated with the different groups who lived in the West from 1870–1900.

Lunch
- ☐ Construct a scrapbook of primary and secondary sources that share different opinions about the Transcontinental Railroad. Record a brief analysis of each source included.
- ☐ Create a class game in which players experience the benefits and drawbacks of the completion of the Transcontinental Railroad.
- ☐ Write an essay that discusses the political, social, and economic impacts of the Transcontinental Railroad through the 1950s.

Dinner
- ☐ Prepare a student-taught lesson that analyzes the impacts of key papers or books written during this time.
- ☐ Record a documentary that investigates the connection between *A Century of Dishonor* and the Dawes Act, as well as the act's impact on tribal lands today.
- ☐ Create a visual product that compares Turner's view of the Frontier with more modern views.

Dessert
- ☐ **Free choice on the West**—Prepare a proposal form and submit it to your teacher for approval.
- ☐ Research museums (and their exhibits) that focus on this period. Create a product that critiques at least two exhibits, sharing changes you would propose, even proposing key aspects of an exhibit you would design.

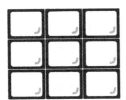

The Second Industrial Revolution

Game Show Menu

Objectives Covered Through This Menu and These Activities

- Students will discuss the political, economic, and social events and issues related to the inventions, entrepreneurs, immigration, and urban developments associated with the Second Industrial Revolution.
- Students will create written, oral, and visual presentations of social studies information using effective communication skills, including proper citations and avoiding plagiarism.
- Students will use critical thinking skills and a variety of primary and secondary source material to explain and apply different methods that historians use to understand and interpret the past, including multiple points of view and historical context.
- Students will analyze information by applying absolute and relative chronology.
- Students will describe the relationship between the arts and popular culture and the times during which they were created.
- Students will analyze the impact of technological innovations on American life.

Materials Needed by Students for Completion

- Poster board or large white paper
- Recording software or application (for videos, documentaries)
- Materials for board games (folders, colored cards, etc.)
- Materials for three-dimensional timelines
- Recycled materials (for museum exhibits)
- Materials for bulletin board display
- Blank index cards (for trading cards)

Special Notes on the Use of This Menu

- This menu gives students the opportunity to create a video and documentary. The grading and sharing of these products can often be facilitated by having students prerecord their product using whatever technology is most convenient for the teacher. This allows the teacher to decide when it will be shown as well as keeps the presentation to its intended length. If recording options are limited, this activity can be modified by allowing students to act out the product (like a play) in front of the class.

- This menu asks students to use recycled materials to create their museum exhibit. This does not mean only plastic and paper; instead, students should focus on using materials in new ways. It works well if a box is started for "recycled" contributions at the beginning of the school year. That way, students always have access to these types of materials.

- This menu allows students to create a bulletin board display. Some classrooms may only have one bulletin board, so the teacher can divide the board into sections, or additional classroom wall or hall space can be sectioned off for the creation of these displays. Students can plan their display based on the amount of space they are assigned.

- This menu allows students to create a WebQuest. There are multiple versions and templates for WebQuests available on the Internet. It is your decision whether you would like to specify a format or if you will allow students to create one of their own choosing.

- This menu provides the students the option of creating a visual presentation or product. This term has been included on the product guidelines, but it refers to students having a choice of what type of visual product they would like to create. On the product guidelines, they will find a short list, but they are welcome to propose other web-based or tangible options.

Time Frame

- 2–3 weeks—Students are given their menu as the unit is started, and the guidelines and point expectations on the back of the menu are discussed. As lessons are taught throughout the unit, students and the teacher can refer back to the options associated with that topic (or column). The teacher will go over all of the options for the topic being covered and have students place checkmarks in the boxes next to the activities they are most interested in completing. As teaching continues over the next 2–3 weeks, activities are discussed, chosen, and submitted for grading.

- 1 week—At the beginning of the unit, the teacher chooses an activity from each area they feel would be most valuable for students. Stations can be set up in the classroom or one of the teacher-selected activities could be provided each day for completion. These activities are available for student choice throughout the week as regular instruction takes place.

- 1–2 days—The teacher chooses an activity from an objective to use with the entire class during that lesson time.

Suggested Forms

- All-purpose rubric
- Proposal form for point-based products
- Presentation rubric

Guidelines for the Second Industrial Revolution Game Show Menu

- You must choose at least one activity from each topic area.
- You may not do more than two activities in any one topic area for credit. (You are, of course, welcome to do more than two for your own investigation.)
- Grading will be ongoing, so turn in products as you complete them.
- All free-choice proposals must be turned in and approved *prior* to working on the free choice.
- You must earn **120** points for a 100%. You may earn extra credit up to _____ points.
- You must show your teacher your plan for completion by: _____.

The Second Industrial Revolution

Inventions	Entrepreneurs	Unions and Strikes	Immigration	Urban Development	Points for Each Level
☐ Make a mind map to share the different types and uses of inventions developed during this time. (10 pts.)	☐ Fold a folded quiz book about the different entrepreneurs and their impact in this time. (10 pts.)	☐ Create a flipbook that compares the different unions and shares information about important strikes. (10 pts.)	☐ Develop a bulletin board display that shows the common pathways of immigration from different home countries to locations in the U.S. (15 pts.)	☐ Assemble a set of trading cards for the different social reform movements and urban developments during this time. (15 pts.)	10–15 points
☐ Record a video that discusses the most important invention of this time as well as its impact through history. (25 pts.)	☐ Construct a board game in which players follow the path to wealth followed by entrepreneurs in the 1860s. (25 pts.)	☐ Assemble a three-dimensional timeline that shows the development and impact of the unions as well as the impact of significant strikes. (20 pts.)	☐ Using primary and secondary sources, draw a Venn diagram to compare the image of the U.S. with the realities immigrants experienced. (20 pts.)	☐ Design an advertisement to support one of the urban reform movements during this time. (20 pts.)	20–25 points
☐ Thomas Edison is known for many inventions, some that were patented but never built. Select one such invention and create a poster to share the machine and its potential impact on society had it been produced. (30 pts.)	☐ Andrew Carnegie and John D. Rockefeller had two quite different views on society. Prepare a You Be the Person presentation in which you come to class and interact with classmates as one of these people. (30 pts.)	☐ Compare the impact of unions and strikes during this time with current times. Build a museum exhibit that shows how they have developed through present day. (30 pts.)	☐ Prepare a product of your choice that shares how the immigrant experience was expressed through art, music, or literature during this time. (30 pts.)	☐ Which urban development has had the most impact on the modern day? Record a documentary in which you track its development from the late 1800s to present day. (30 pts.)	30 points
Free Choice (prior approval) (10–30 pts.)	**Free Choice** (prior approval) (10–30 pts.)	**Free Choice** (prior approval) (10–30 pts.)	**Free Choice** (prior approval) (10–30 pts.)	**Free Choice** (prior approval) (10–30 pts.)	10–30 points
Total:	**Total:**	**Total:**	**Total:**	**Total:**	**Total Grade:**

```
┌─────────────────┐
│ 20 Points       │
│ ▫ _____      │
│ ▫ _____      │
│ 50 Points       │
│ ▫ _____      │
│ ▫ _____      │
│ ▫ _____      │
│ ▫ _____      │
│ 80 Points       │
│ ▫ _____      │
│ ▫ _____      │
└─────────────────┘
```

The Progressive Era

20-50-80 Menu

Objectives Covered Through This Menu and These Activities

- Students will discuss the political, economic, and social events and issues related to the Progressive Era.
- Students will create visual representations of historical information.
- Students will use a variety of rich primary and secondary source material.
- Students will analyze the impact of technological innovations on American life.

Materials Needed by Students for Completion

- Poster board or large white paper
- Magazines (for collages)
- Blank index cards (for concentration cards)
- Recording software or application (for videos, reenactments)

Special Notes on the Use of This Menu

- This menu gives students the opportunity to create a video and record a reenactment. The grading and sharing of these products can often be facilitated by having students prerecord their product using whatever technology is most convenient for the teacher. This allows the teacher to decide when it will be shown as well as keeps the presentation to its intended length. If recording options are limited, this activity can be modified by allowing students to act out the product (like a play) in front of the class.
- This menu gives students the opportunity to teach a concept. This can take a significant amount of time and organization. It can save time if the students who choose to do a lesson can sign up for a designated day and time that is determined when the menu is distributed.

Time Frame

- 1–2 weeks—Students are given a menu as the unit is started, and the teacher discusses all of the product options on the menu. As the different options are discussed, students will choose the activities they are most interested in completing so that they meet their goal of 100 points. As the lessons progress through the week(s), the teacher and students refer back to the menu options associated with the content being taught.

- 1–2 days—The teacher chooses an activity or product from the menu to use with the entire class.

Suggested Forms

- All-purpose rubric
- Proposal form for point-based projects
- Presentation rubric
- Student-taught lesson rubric

Name:_____ Date:_____

The Progressive Era

Directions: Choose at least two activities from the menu below. The activities must total 100 points. Place a checkmark next to each box to show which activities you will complete. All activities must be completed by _____ .

---

20 Points

- ☐ Develop a collage with pictures that represent the different political and social events of the Progressive Era.

- ☐ Assemble a set of concentration cards in which players match different political and social events with their impacts.

---

50 Points

- ☐ Using primary and secondary sources, prepare and record a reenactment of the Seneca Falls Convention.

- ☐ Use primary and secondary sources as references to write an original newspaper article about President Theodore Roosevelt's impact on the conservation of public lands.

- ☐ Muckrakers played a significant role during this era, but what about in present day? Draw a Venn diagram to compare the work of the muckrakers of the Progressive Era and modern day.

- ☐ **Free choice on the impacts of the Progressive Era**—Prepare a proposal form and submit it to your teacher for approval.

---

80 Points

- ☐ Historians often note that the availability of and access to natural resources defined this era. Record a video in which you investigate and provide evidence of this statement.

- ☐ Prepare a student-taught lesson about the most *socially* impactful event of the Progressive Era. Your lesson should provide opportunities to discuss the event and its impact throughout history.

Imperialism and World War I

Four-Topic List Menu

Objectives Covered Through This Menu and These Activities

- Students will discuss the political, economic, and social events and issues related to imperialism and World War I.
- Students will create written, oral, and visual presentations of social studies information using effective communication skills, including proper citations and avoiding plagiarism.
- Students will use a variety of rich primary and secondary source material.
- Students will apply the process of historical inquiry to research, interpret, and use multiple types of sources of evidence.
- Students will describe the relationship between the arts and popular culture and the times during which they were created.

Materials Needed by Students for Completion

- Poster board or large white paper
- Blank index cards (for card sorts)
- Magazines (for collages)
- Microsoft PowerPoint or other slideshow software

Special Notes on the Use of This Menu

- This menu provides the students the option of creating a visual presentation or product. This term has been included on the product guidelines, but it refers to students having a choice of what type of visual product they would like to create. On the product guidelines, they will find a short list, but they are welcome to propose other web-based or tangible options.

Time Frame

- 1–2 weeks—Students are given the menu as the unit is started, and the guidelines and point expectations are discussed. Students usually will need to earn 100 points for 100%, although there is an opportunity for extra credit if the teacher would like to use another target number. Because this menu covers one topic in depth, the teacher will go over all of the options for the topic being covered and have

students place checkmarks in the boxes next to the activities they are most interested in completing. Teachers will need to set aside a few moments to sign the agreement at the bottom of the page with each student. As instruction continues, activities are completed by students and submitted to the teacher for grading.
- 1–2 days—The teacher chooses an activity or product from an objective to use with the entire class during that lesson time.

Suggested Forms
- All-purpose rubric
- Proposal form for point-based products
- Presentation rubric

Name:_____ Date:_____

Imperialism and World War I

Guidelines:
1. You may complete as many of the activities listed as you wish within the time period.
2. You may choose any combination of activities, but **must** complete at least one activity from each topic area.
3. Your goal is 120 points. (This is a grade of 100/100.) You may earn up to _____ points extra credit.
4. You may be as creative as you like within the guidelines listed below.
5. You must show your plan to your teacher by _____ .
6. Activities may be turned in at any time during the working time period. They will be graded and recorded on this sheet as you continue to work, so keep it safe!

Topic	Plan to Do	Activity to Complete	Point Value	Date Completed	Points Earned
Imperialism		Make a card sort to practice sorting historical events that represent Manifest Destiny and imperialism.	15		
		Draw a windowpane that shows different examples of imperialism from 1900 to present day.	20		
		Locate at least two political cartoons from primary or secondary sources that represent imperialism during this time. Create a PowerPoint presentation with the two cartoons and your analyses of the cartoons.	25		
		Using the philosophies of imperialism, record a speech you could have given to support one of the presidential actions of the time.	25		
The Spanish-American War		Draw a T-chart to share how lands were controlled before and after the Spanish-American War.	15		
		Assemble a collage of primary and secondary source examples of yellow journalism from this time. Include an explanation for each.	20		
		Prepare a poster that shares the most important economic impact of the Spanish-American War.	20		
		Research the outcomes of the Spanish-American War on the Philippines and Cuba. Write an essay that discusses the political and economic reasons for the different outcomes for each country.	25		
The Road to World War I		Write Three Facts and a Fib about the naval impact of the U.S. declaring war on Germany.	15		
		Make an acrostic for the term *World War I*. Record popular thoughts about the war for each letter.	20		
		Using the art of this time, prepare a visual product that shares the events that led up to U.S. involvement in World War I.	20		
		Create a social media profile for a Social Darwinist considering the development of the Committee on Public Information.	25		
The U.S. in World War I		Write a folded quiz book about the causes and consequences of the Great Migration.	15		
		Prepare a mind map that shows the different political actions during World War I and the associated impacts of each.	20		
		Design an advertisement that the Committee on Public Information could have used to rally public support.	25		
		Write a Choose Your Own Adventure story in which the reader may experience the effects of the Espionage and Sedition Acts.	30		

Name:_____ Date:_____

Topic	Plan to Do	Activity to Complete	Point Value	Date Completed	Points Earned
Any		**Free Choice:** Submit your free-choice proposal form for a product of your choice.			
		Total number of points you are planning to earn.		**Total points earned:**	

I am planning to complete _____ activities that could earn up to a total of _____ points.

Teacher's initials _____ Student's signature _____

The Roaring 20s

Tic-Tac-Toe Menu

Objectives Covered Through This Menu and These Activities
- Students will discuss the political, economic, and social events and issues related to the Roaring 20s and the Harlem Renaissance.
- Students will create visual representations of historical information.
- Students will use critical thinking skills and a variety of primary and secondary source material to explain and apply different methods that historians use to understand and interpret the past, including multiple points of view and historical context.
- Students will describe the relationship between the arts and popular culture and the times during which they were created.
- Students will analyze the impact of technological innovations on American life.

Materials Needed by Students for Completion
- Poster board or large white paper
- Blank index cards (for trading cards)
- Recording software or application (for videos)

Special Notes on the Use of This Menu
- This menu gives students the opportunity to create a video. The grading and sharing of these products can often be facilitated by having students prerecord their product using whatever technology is most convenient for the teacher. This allows the teacher to decide when it will be shown as well as keeps the presentation to its intended length. If recording options are limited, this activity can be modified by allowing students to act out the product (like a play) in front of the class.
- This menu gives students the opportunity to teach a concept. This can take a significant amount of time and organization. It can save time if the students who choose to do a lesson can sign up for a designated day and time that is determined when the menu is distributed.
- This menu provides the students the option of creating a visual presentation or product. This term has been included on the product guidelines, but it refers to students having a choice of what type of visual product they would like to create. On the product guidelines,

they will find a short list, but they are welcome to propose other web-based or tangible options.

Time Frame

- 2–3 weeks—Students are given the menu as the unit is started. The teacher will go over all of the options for that content and have students place checkmarks in the boxes that represent the activities they are most interested in completing. As students choose activities, they should complete a column or a row. When students complete this pattern, they have completed one activity from each content area, learning style, or level of Bloom's revised taxonomy, depending on the design of the menu. As the teacher presents lessons throughout the week, they should refer back to the menu options associated with that content.
- 1 week—At the start of the unit, the teacher chooses the three activities they feel are most valuable for students. Stations can be set up in the classroom. These three activities are available for student choice throughout the week as regular instruction takes place.
- 1–2 days—The teacher chooses an activity from the menu to use with the entire class.

Suggested Forms

- All-purpose rubric
- Free-choice proposal form
- Presentation rubric
- Student-taught lesson rubric

The Roaring 20s

Directions: Check the boxes you plan to complete. They should form a tic-tac-toe across or down. All products are due by: _____ .

☐ *The Economy*	☐ *The Politics and Society*	☐ *The Arts*
There were great advances during this era that allowed average families to afford higher priced items. Research the changes made during this time and create a brochure that explains these options to the average family.	The 1920 presidential election impacted society in the 1920s. To better understand the impact, organize a mock debate between the two 1920 presidential candidates as they seek to become president. Be prepared to ask and answer tough questions from the audience about their policies.	Analyze primary and secondary source literary reviews for at least two Lost Generation novelists. Use that information to write a children's book about the political and social impacts of their works.
☐ *The Arts*	☐ **Free Choice: The Economy** (Fill out your proposal form before beginning the free choice!)	☐ *The Politics and Society*
Create a student-taught lesson on the Harlem Renaissance writers and artists of the 1920s. Include the inspirations for their work as well as how their work inspired others in the 1920s and beyond.		The 19th Amendment was ratified in 1920. Prepare a visual presentation to share its political and societal impacts in this decade.
☐ *The Politics and Society*	☐ *The Arts*	☐ *The Economy*
Each president in this decade directly impacted society. Create a set of trading cards that details each president, their platform, and their political and societal impacts.	Investigate the art and music movements of this time. Record a video of works created during this time, including the Harlem Renaissance, as well as present-day works that reflect the style of the 1920s. You can also create your own piece of art to add to your presentation.	Research the millionaires of the Roaring 20s and how they earned their money. Write a story that shares how an average family became millionaires during the 1920s.

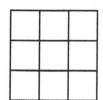

The Great Depression and the New Deals

Tic-Tac-Toe Menu

Objectives Covered Through This Menu and These Activities

- Students will discuss the political, economic, and social events and issues related to the Great Depression and the New Deals.
- Students will create written, oral, and visual presentations of social studies information using effective communication skills, including proper citations and avoiding plagiarism.
- Students will apply the process of historical inquiry to research, interpret, and use multiple types of sources of evidence.
- Students will describe how the characteristics of and issues in U.S. history have been reflected in various genres of art, music, and literature.

Materials Needed by Students for Completion

- Poster board or large white paper
- Recording software or application (for commercials)
- Blank index cards (for trading cards)

Special Notes on the Use of This Menu

- This menu gives students the opportunity to create a commercial. The grading and sharing of these products can often be facilitated by having students prerecord their product using whatever technology is most convenient for the teacher. This allows the teacher to decide when it will be shown as well as keeps the presentation to its intended length. If recording options are limited, this activity can be modified by allowing students to act out the product (like a play) in front of the class.
- This menu gives students the opportunity to teach a concept. This can take a significant amount of time and organization. It can save time if the students who choose to do a lesson can sign up for a designated day and time that is determined when the menu is distributed.
- This menu provides the students the option of creating a visual presentation or product. This term has been included on the product guidelines, but it refers to students having a choice of what type of visual product they would like to create. On the product guidelines,

they will find a short list, but they are welcome to propose other web-based or tangible options.

Time Frame

- 2–3 weeks—Students are given the menu as the unit is started. The teacher will go over all of the options for that content and have students place checkmarks in the boxes that represent the activities they are most interested in completing. As students choose activities, they should complete a column or a row. When students complete this pattern, they have completed one activity from each content area, learning style, or level of Bloom's revised taxonomy, depending on the design of the menu. As the teacher presents lessons throughout the week, they should refer back to the menu options associated with that content.
- 1 week—At the start of the unit, the teacher chooses the three activities they feel are most valuable for students. Stations can be set up in the classroom. These three activities are available for student choice throughout the week as regular instruction takes place.
- 1–2 days—The teacher chooses an activity from the menu to use with the entire class.

Suggested Forms

- All-purpose rubric
- Free-choice proposal form
- Presentation rubric
- Student-taught lesson rubric

Name:_____ Date:_____

The Great Depression and the New Deals

Directions: Check the boxes you plan to complete. They should form a tic-tac-toe across or down. All products are due by: _____ .

☐ *The Great Depression* Create an obituary for a farmer who survived the Great Depression.	☐ *The New Deal* Record a commercial that could have been used to recruit workers for the Public Works Administration or the Civilian Conservation Corps.	☐ *The Second New Deal* President Franklin D. Roosevelt implemented additional reforms advocated by different reformers. Assemble a set of trading cards for the reformers who proposed key aspects of the Second New Deal.
☐ *The Second New Deal* Prepare a student-taught lesson about Second New Deal outcomes that impact our daily lives.	☐ **Free Choice:** **The Great Depression** (Fill out your proposal form before beginning the free choice!)	☐ *The New Deal* Make a map (with explanation of locations) that shows the impact of the Civilian Conservation Corps throughout the U.S.
☐ *The New Deal* Select a piece of art, music, or literature you feel best represents society's feelings about the implementation of the New Deal legislations. Share your selection and explanation through a visual product of your choice.	☐ *The Second New Deal* If all of the initiatives of the Second New Deal were put into a book in 1935, what would be the best title of the book? Design a book cover for this book.	☐ *The Great Depression* Design a social media profile for a banker during the Great Depression.

World War II

Meal Menu

Objectives Covered Through This Menu and These Activities
- Students will discuss the political, economic, and social events and issues related to World War II.
- Students will create written, oral, and visual presentations of social studies information using effective communication skills, including proper citations and avoiding plagiarism.
- Students will apply the process of historical inquiry to research, interpret, and use multiple types of sources of evidence.
- Students will describe how the characteristics of and issues in U.S. history have been reflected in various genres of art, music, and literature.

Materials Needed by Students for Completion
- Poster board or large white paper
- Recording software or application (for videos)
- Scrapbooking materials (or electronic portfolios)
- Graph paper or Internet access (for WebQuests)

Special Notes on the Use of This Menu
- This menu gives students the opportunity to create a video. The grading and sharing of these products can often be facilitated by having students prerecord their product using whatever technology is most convenient for the teacher. This allows the teacher to decide when it will be shown as well as keeps the presentation to its intended length. If recording options are limited, this activity can be modified by allowing students to act out the product (like a play) in front of the class.
- This menu gives students the opportunity to facilitate a class model. The expectation is that all students in the classroom will play an active role in the model. This may mean that students need some additional space for their model.
- This menu allows students to create a WebQuest. There are multiple versions and templates for WebQuests available on the Internet. It is your decision whether you would like to specify a format or if you will allow students to create one of their own choosing.

- This menu provides the students the option of creating a visual presentation or product. This term has been included on the product guidelines, but it refers to students having a choice of what type of visual product they would like to create. On the product guidelines, they will find a short list, but they are welcome to propose other web-based or tangible options.

Time Frame

- 2–3 weeks—Students are given the menu as the unit is started. As the lesson or unit progresses throughout the week, students should refer to the menu options associated with that content. The teacher will go over all of the options for that objective and have students place a checkmark in the box for each option that represents the activity they are most interested in completing. As teaching continues, the activities chosen and completed should create a full day's meal, with a breakfast, a lunch, and a dinner. The teacher may choose to allow students time to work after other work is finished. When students complete the menu with this expectation, they have completed one activity from each content area, learning style, or level of Bloom's revised taxonomy, depending on the design of the menu.
- 1 week—At the start of the unit, the teacher chooses one activity from each meal family they feel are most valuable for students. Stations can be set up in the classroom. These three activities are available for student choice throughout the week as regular instruction takes place.
- 1–2 days—The teacher chooses an activity or product from an objective to use with the entire class during that lesson time. Additionally, the teacher could choose one of the two desserts as an enrichment activity.

Suggested Forms

- All-purpose rubric
- Free-choice proposal form
- Presentation rubric

World War II

Directions: Choose one activity each for breakfast, lunch, and dinner. Dessert is an activity you can choose to do after you have finished your other meals. All products must be completed by: _____ .

Breakfast

❒ Create a visual product that shares the members of the League of Nations and their reasons for joining.

❒ Write Three Facts and a Fib about membership in the League of Nations.

❒ Make a blog that could have been used at the time to keep the members of the League of Nations informed about the League's actions.

Lunch

❒ Consider the Leagues of Nation's response to Mussolini's actions. Write an essay in which you hypothesize a different response and its impact on history.

❒ Draw a mind map that shows the connections between the League of Nations and the drawing of the U.S. into World War II.

❒ Propose a class model that demonstrates the various actions that led to the U.S. declaring war on Japan.

Dinner

❒ Record a video to share the social and economic impacts of World War II on different groups of people in the U.S.

❒ Create a social media profile for a woman, African American, or Japanese American during World War II.

❒ Select at least four political cartoons that you feel best represent different aspects of World War II. Assemble a scrapbook with these cartoons and your defense for selecting them.

Dessert

❒ **Free choice on World War II**—Prepare a proposal form and submit it to your teacher for approval.

❒ Prepare a WebQuest that allows users to experience the art, music, and literature of this time.

The Cold
War Through
Present Day

The Cold War

Tic-Tac-Toe Menu

Objectives Covered Through This Menu and These Activities

- Students will discuss the political, economic, and social events and issues related to the Cold War.
- Students will create written, oral, and visual presentations of social studies information using effective communication skills, including proper citations and avoiding plagiarism.
- Students will use critical thinking skills and a variety of primary and secondary source material to explain and apply different methods that historians use to understand and interpret the past, including multiple points of view and historical context.

Materials Needed by Students for Completion

- Poster board or large white paper
- Recording software or application (for documentaries, videos)

Special Notes on the Use of This Menu

- This menu gives students the opportunity to create a video or documentary. The grading and sharing of these products can often be facilitated by having students prerecord their product using whatever technology is most convenient for the teacher. This allows the teacher to decide when it will be shown as well as keeps the presentation to its intended length. If recording options are limited, this activity can be modified by allowing students to act out the product (like a play) in front of the class.
- This menu provides the students the option of creating a visual presentation or product. This term has been included on the product guidelines, but it refers to students having a choice of what type of visual product they would like to create. On the product guidelines, they will find a short list, but they are welcome to propose other web-based or tangible options.

Time Frame

- 2–3 weeks—Students are given the menu as the unit is started. The teacher will go over all of the options for that content and have students place checkmarks in the boxes that represent the activities they are most interested in completing. As students choose activities, they should complete a column or a row. When students complete this pattern, they have completed one activity from each content area, learning style, or level of Bloom's revised taxonomy, depending on the design of the menu. As the teacher presents lessons throughout the week, they should refer back to the menu options associated with that content.

- 1 week—At the start of the unit, the teacher chooses the three activities they feel are most valuable for students. Stations can be set up in the classroom. These three activities are available for student choice throughout the week as regular instruction takes place.
- 1–2 days—The teacher chooses an activity from the menu to use with the entire class.

Suggested Forms

- All-purpose rubric
- Free-choice proposal form
- Presentation rubric

The Cold War

Directions: Check the boxes you plan to complete. They should form a tic-tac-toe across or down. All products are due by: _____ .

☐ *Causes of the Cold War* The U.S. and Russia emerged from World War II differently. Record a documentary in which you address the impact of World War II and the initiation of the Cold War from each perspective.	☐ *The Containment Policy: Truman Doctrine* Make a flipbook that shares at least seven future political decisions based on Truman's Doctrine. Include the outcome of each decision.	☐ *The Korean War* Prepare a fictitious interview with President Harry S. Truman about his decision to not ask Congress to declare war on North Korea.
☐ *The Korean War* Create a visual product that illustrates the importance of the 38th parallel to those who were both North and South of its demarcation.	☐ **Free Choice: Causes of the Cold War** (Fill out your proposal form before beginning the free choice!)	☐ *The Containment Policy: Marshall Plan* Write Three Facts and a Fib about the political and economic impacts of the Marshall Plan on Russia.
☐ *The Containment Policy: North Atlantic Treaty Organization* Draw a Venn diagram to compare the North Atlantic Treaty and the Warsaw Pact.	☐ *The Korean War* Draw two original political cartoons about the social impacts of the Korean War—one that would have been drawn in 1948 and one that could be drawn today.	☐ *Causes of the Cold War* Henry Wallace provided advice about dealing with the Russian containment actions. Record a video in which you hypothesize the historical impacts of following his advice.

The 1950s

Three-Topic List Menu

Objectives Covered Through This Menu and These Activities

- Students will discuss the political, economic, and social events and issues related to the 1950s.
- Students will create written, oral, and visual presentations of social studies information using effective communication skills, including proper citations and avoiding plagiarism.
- Students will create visual representations of historical information.
- Students will apply the process of historical inquiry to research, interpret, and use multiple types of sources of evidence.
- Students will analyze information by applying absolute and relative chronology.
- Students will describe how the characteristics of and issues in U.S. history have been reflected in various genres of art, music, and literature.

Materials Needed by Students for Completion

- Poster board or large white paper
- Magazines (for collages)
- Graph paper or Internet access (for WebQuests)
- Recording software or application (for videos)
- Blank index cards (for trading cards)
- Materials for three-dimensional timelines

Special Notes on the Use of This Menu

- This menu gives students the opportunity to create a video. The grading and sharing of these products can often be facilitated by having students prerecord their product using whatever technology is most convenient for the teacher. This allows the teacher to decide when it will be shown as well as keeps the presentation to its intended length. If recording options are limited, this activity can be modified by allowing students to act out the product (like a play) in front of the class.
- This menu allows students to create a WebQuest. There are multiple versions and templates for WebQuests available on the Internet. It is your decision whether you would like to specify a format or if you will allow students to create one of their own choosing.

- This menu provides the students the option of creating a visual presentation or product. This term has been included on the product guidelines, but it refers to students having a choice of what type of visual product they would like to create. On the product guidelines, they will find a short list, but they are welcome to propose other web-based or tangible options.

Time Frame

- 1–2 weeks—Students are given the menu as the unit is started, and the guidelines and point expectations are discussed. Students usually will need to earn 100 points for 100%, although there is an opportunity for extra credit if the teacher would like to use another target number. Because this menu covers one topic in depth, the teacher will go over all of the options for the topic being covered and have students place checkmarks in the boxes next to the activities they are most interested in completing. Teachers will need to set aside a few moments to sign the agreement at the bottom of the page with each student. As instruction continues, activities are completed by students and submitted to the teacher for grading.
- 1–2 days—The teacher chooses an activity or product from an objective to use with the entire class during that lesson time.

Suggested Forms

- All-purpose rubric
- Proposal form for point-based products
- Presentation rubric

Name:_____ Date:_____

The 1950s

Guidelines:
1. You may complete as many of the activities listed as you wish within the time period.
2. You may choose any combination of activities, but **must** complete at least one activity from each topic area.
3. Your goal is 100 points. (This is a grade of 100/100.) You may earn up to _____ points extra credit.
4. You may be as creative as you like within the guidelines listed below.
5. You must show your plan to your teacher by _____ .
6. Activities may be turned in at any time during the working time period. They will be graded and recorded on this sheet as you continue to work, so keep it safe!

Topic	Plan to Do	Activity to Complete	Point Value	Date Completed	Points Earned
Culture		Use birthrate data from 1940–1950 to create a graph. Post your graph with a brief explanation for the observed trends.	15		
		Assemble a collage that represents different key social aspects of this time.	15		
		Create a product of your choice that shares the societal impact of art and music during this time.	20		
		Prepare a WebQuest that allows questors to experience domesticity during the 50s.	25		
		Would you like living in the 50s? Record a video in which you discuss your thoughts about 50s culture.	25		
The Rebels		Draw an outline of a "beat." Label different parts of the drawing with different aspects of their beliefs.	15		
		Assemble a set of trading cards for the social critics who spoke out or wrote against the societal changes during the 50s.	20		
		Research the artistic movements in the 50s. Create a visual product that shares key works and their presentation of the 50s culture.	25		
		Create a list of song titles that represent those who rebelled against the suburban domesticated life.	25		
The Civil Rights Movement		Draw a windowpane that shows different forms of nonviolent civil disobedience.	15		
		Build a three-dimensional civil rights timeline that begins with *Brown v. Board of Education*.	20		
		Write and record a song about Dr. Martin Luther King, Jr.'s message of nonviolent civil disobedience.	25		
		Create a website or blog that may have been published during this time to unite Americans in King's cause.	25		
Any		**Free Choice:** Submit your free-choice proposal form for a product of your choice.			
		Total number of points you are planning to earn.		**Total points earned:**	

I am planning to complete _____ activities that could earn up to a total of _____ points.

Teacher's initials _____ Student's signature _____

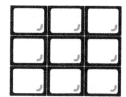

The 1960s and 1970s

Game Show Menu

Objectives Covered Through This Menu and These Activities

- Students will discuss the political, economic, and social events and issues related to the 1960s and 1970s.
- Students will create written, oral, and visual presentations of social studies information using effective communication skills, including proper citations and avoiding plagiarism.
- Students will use critical thinking skills and a variety of primary and secondary source material to explain and apply different methods that historians use to understand and interpret the past, including multiple points of view and historical context.
- Students will analyze information by applying absolute and relative chronology.
- Students will apply the process of historical inquiry to research, interpret, and use multiple types of sources of evidence.
- Students will describe the relationship between the arts and popular culture and the times during which they were created.

Materials Needed by Students for Completion

- Poster board or large white paper
- Materials for three-dimensional timelines
- Recording software or application (for videos)
- Magazines (for collages)
- Graph paper or Internet access (for crossword puzzles, WebQuests)
- Blank index cards (for card sorts)

Special Notes on the Use of This Menu

- This menu gives students the opportunity to create a video. The grading and sharing of these products can often be facilitated by having students prerecord their product using whatever technology is most convenient for the teacher. This allows the teacher to decide when it will be shown as well as keeps the presentation to its intended length. If recording options are limited, this activity can be modified by allowing students to act out the product (like a play) in front of the class.
- This menu gives students the opportunity to teach a concept. This can take a significant amount of time and organization. It can save

time if the students who choose to do a lesson can sign up for a designated day and time that is determined when the menu is distributed.

- This menu gives students the opportunity to facilitate a reenactment. The expectation is that all students in the classroom will have an opportunity to participate if possible. This may mean that students need some additional time for their product.
- This menu allows students to create a WebQuest. There are multiple versions and templates for WebQuests available on the Internet. It is your decision whether you would like to specify a format or if you will allow students to create one of their own choosing.
- This menu provides the students the option of creating a visual presentation or product. This term has been included on the product guidelines, but it refers to students having a choice of what type of visual product they would like to create. On the product guidelines, they will find a short list, but they are welcome to propose other web-based or tangible options.

Time Frame

- 2–3 weeks—Students are given their menu as the unit is started, and the guidelines and point expectations on the back of the menu are discussed. As lessons are taught throughout the unit, students and the teacher can refer back to the options associated with that topic (or column). The teacher will go over all of the options for the topic being covered and have students place checkmarks in the boxes next to the activities they are most interested in completing. As teaching continues over the next 2–3 weeks, activities are discussed, chosen, and submitted for grading.
- 1 week—At the beginning of the unit, the teacher chooses an activity from each area they feel would be most valuable for students. Stations can be set up in the classroom or one of the teacher-selected activities could be provided each day for completion. These activities are available for student choice throughout the week as regular instruction takes place.
- 1–2 days—The teacher chooses an activity from an objective to use with the entire class during that lesson time.

Suggested Forms

- All-purpose rubric
- Student-taught lesson rubric
- Proposal form for point-based products
- Presentation rubric

Name:_____ Date:_____

Guidelines for the 1960s and 1970s Game Show Menu

- You must choose at least one activity from each topic area.
- You may not do more than two activities in any one topic area for credit. (You are, of course, welcome to do more than two for your own investigation.)
- Grading will be ongoing, so turn in products as you complete them.
- All free-choice proposals must be turned in and approved *prior* to working on the free choice.
- You must earn **150** points for a 100%. You may earn extra credit up to _____ points.
- You must show your teacher your plan for completion by: _____.

Name:_____ Date:_____

The 1960s and 1970s

The Cold War	The Civil Rights Movement	The Great Society	The Vietnam War	The Feminist Movement	The Carter Presidency	Points for Each Level
☐ Build a three-dimensional timeline to detail the significant Cold War events during this period. (15 pts.)	☐ Make an acrostic for the term *Civil Rights Movement*. Record statements and beliefs for each letter. (10 pts.)	☐ Assemble a collage to represent President Lyndon B. Johnson's view of a Great Society. (15 pts.)	☐ Invent a crossword puzzle for the social and political aspects of the Vietnam War during this period. (15 pts.)	☐ Write Three Facts and a Fib about the Feminist Movement of this time. (15 pts.)	☐ Develop a card sort of events during President Jimmy Carter's term that positively and negatively impacted his reelection. (15 pts.)	10–15 points
☐ Locate at least two primary sources for a the Cold War engagement during this time. Write journal entries from the perspective of a soldier involved in that engagement. (20 pts.)	☐ Create a Venn diagram to compare John F. Kennedy's and Lyndon Johnson's political and societal impact on the Civil Rights Movement. (25 pts.)	☐ Write and record a speech introducing and supporting one of Johnson's Great Society initiatives. (25 pts.)	☐ Locate at least three political cartoons that examine the views of hawks versus doves. Create a scrapbook to share the cartoons and your analyses of each. (25 pts.)	☐ Design a social media profile for a woman who wants advice on joining the National Organization for Women. (25 pts.)	☐ Create a political campaign advertisement that Carter could have used for his 1980 campaign. (25 pts.)	20–25 points
☐ Which president who served during these 20 years had the largest impact on the Cold War? Record a video in which you describe the social, political, and economic reasons for your choice. (30 pts.)	☐ Revisit all of the amendments that have impacted civil rights. Prepare a student-taught lesson about the history and impact of these amendments on society. (30 pts.)	☐ Write an essay in which you evaluate the value of the different programs Johnson implemented during his time in office as well as their impact today. (30 pts.)	☐ Record a news report that questions the relationship between The Gulf of Tonkin Resolution and presidential power. (30 pts.)	☐ Prepare a WebQuest to let questors experience the messages of the different feminist groups during this time through primary sources. (30 pts.)	☐ Prepare a reenactment of Carter's Camp David Accords. Base your reenactment on primary and secondary sources for accuracy. (30 pts.)	30 points
Free Choice (prior approval) (10–30 pts.)	**Free Choice** (prior approval) (10–30 pts.)	**Free Choice** (prior approval) (10–30 pts.)	**Free Choice** (prior approval) (10–30 pts.)	**Free Choice** (prior approval) (10–30 pts.)	**Free Choice** (prior approval) (10–30 pts.)	10–30 points
Total:	**Total:**	**Total:**	**Total:**	**Total:**	**Total:**	**Total Grade:**

© Prufrock Press Inc. • *Differentiating Instruction With Menus: U.S. History* • Grades 9–12   143

The 1980s: President Reagan

20-50-80 Menu

Objectives Covered Through This Menu and These Activities

- Students will discuss the political, economic, and social events and issues related to Ronald Reagan's presidency.
- Students will create written, oral, and visual presentations of social studies information using effective communication skills, including proper citations and avoiding plagiarism.
- Students will use a variety of rich primary and secondary source material.
- Students will identify bias and support with historical evidence.
- Students will describe how the characteristics of and issues in U.S. history have been reflected in various genres of film and literature.

Materials Needed by Students for Completion

- Poster board or large white paper
- Scrapbooking materials (or electronic portfolios)
- Recording software or application (for commercials, videos, news reports)

Special Notes on the Use of This Menu

- This menu gives students the opportunity to create a video. The grading and sharing of these products can often be facilitated by having students prerecord their product using whatever technology is most convenient for the teacher. This allows the teacher to decide when it will be shown as well as keeps the presentation to its intended length. If recording options are limited, this activity can be modified by allowing students to act out the product (like a play) in front of the class.
- This menu provides the students the option of creating a visual presentation or product. This term has been included on the product guidelines, but it refers to students having a choice of what type of visual product they would like to create. On the product guidelines, they will find a short list, but they are welcome to propose other web-based or tangible options.

Time Frame

- 1–2 weeks—Students are given a menu as the unit is started, and the teacher discusses all of the product options on the menu. As the different options are discussed, students will choose the activities they are most interested in completing so that they meet their goal of 100 points. As the lessons progress through the week(s), the teacher and students refer back to the menu options associated with the content being taught.
- 1–2 days—The teacher chooses an activity or product from the menu to use with the entire class.

Suggested Forms

- All-purpose rubric
- Proposal form for point-based projects
- Presentation rubric

The 1980s: President Reagan

Directions: Choose at least two activities from the menu below. The activities must total 100 points. Place a checkmark next to each box to show which activities you will complete. All activities must be completed by _____ .

---

20 Points

❒ Draw a windowpane that shows the different plans implemented by President Ronald Reagan during his presidency.

❒ Write Three Facts and a Fib about Reagan's most significant contribution to present-day politics.

---

50 Points

❒ Make a T-chart to show Reagan's domestic and international political, social, and economic accomplishments.

❒ Decide which speech presented by Reagan had the biggest impact on society. Write an essay that analyzes that speech to determine its effectiveness.

❒ Assemble a scrapbook that could be put on display at the Ronald Reagan Presidential Library and Museum.

❒ **Free choice on Reagan's impact on the 1980s**—Prepare a proposal form and submit it to your teacher for approval.

---

80 Points

❒ Reagan was known to reference a popular movie from this time period when observing other countries. Record a video in which you critique the appropriateness of his use of these movie terms.

❒ Many writers have written biographies about Reagan. Research reviews of these books and select the biography that you feel best represents his presidential impacts in an unbiased way. Prepare a visual product that shares the biography you have selected and evidence from your research to support your choice.

---

20 Points
☐ _____
☐ _____
50 Points
☐ _____
☐ _____
☐ _____
☐ _____
80 Points
☐ _____
☐ _____

Landmark Supreme Court Cases

20-50-80 Menu

Objectives Covered Through This Menu and These Activities

- Students will discuss the political, economic, and social events and issues related to landmark Supreme Court cases.
- Students will create written, oral, and visual presentations of social studies information using effective communication skills, including proper citations and avoiding plagiarism.
- Students will use a variety of rich primary and secondary source material.
- Students will apply the process of historical inquiry to research, interpret, and use multiple types of sources of evidence.
- Students will use social studies terminology correctly.
- Students will examine the impact of geographic factors on major events.

Materials Needed by Students for Completion

- Poster board or large white paper
- Blank index cards (for trading cards, concentration cards)
- Recording software or application (for news reports, informational videos)
- Scrapbooking materials (or electronic portfolios)

Special Notes on the Use of This Menu

- This menu gives students the opportunity to create an informational video or news report. The grading and sharing of these products can often be facilitated by having students prerecord their product using whatever technology is most convenient for the teacher. This allows the teacher to decide when it will be shown as well as keeps the presentation to its intended length. If recording options are limited, this activity can be modified by allowing students to act out the product (like a play) in front of the class.

Time Frame

- 1–2 weeks—Students are given a menu as the unit is started, and the teacher discusses all of the product options on the menu. As the different options are discussed, students will choose the activities they are most interested in completing so that they meet their goal of 100 points. As the lessons progress through the week(s), the teacher and students refer back to the menu options associated with the content being taught.

- 1–2 days—The teacher chooses an activity or product from the menu to use with the entire class.

Suggested Forms

- All-purpose rubric
- Proposal form for point-based projects
- Presentation rubric

Name:_____ Date:_____

Landmark Supreme Court Cases

Directions: Choose at least two activities from the menu below. The activities must total 100 points. Place a checkmark next to each box to show which activities you will complete. All activities must be completed by _____.

20 Points

❒ Create a set of trading cards for the different landmark Supreme Course cases you have identified.

❒ Assemble a set of concentration cards to match landmark Supreme Court cases with their impacts on history.

50 Points

❒ Select a landmark Supreme Court case and record a news report that could have shown at that time sharing the issues behind the case and its significance.

❒ Consider the issues and motivations surrounding a landmark case with economic impacts. Investigate at least three other Supreme Court cases with the same motivations. Design a scrapbook to share the issues and significance of these cases.

❒ After selecting a landmark Supreme Court case, keep a diary as the Chief Justice who presided over it.

❒ **Free choice on landmark Supreme Court cases**—Prepare a proposal form and submit it to your teacher for approval.

80 Points

❒ Select the Supreme Court case you feel has had the most significant impact on today's society. Record an informational video on the motivation behind the case as well as its impact on our country today.

❒ Identify a landmark Supreme Court case that, although not often discussed in U.S. history, has impacted our society today. Prepare a persuasive speech to convince others it should be included in lists of landmark Supreme Court cases.

References

Anderson, L., & Krathwohl, D. R. (Eds.). (2001). *A taxonomy for learning, teaching, and assessing: A revision of Bloom's taxonomy of educational objectives* (Complete ed.). Longman.

Deci, E. L., Vallerand, R. J., Pelletier, L. G., & Ryan, R. M. (1991). Motivation and education: The self-determination perspective. *Educational Psychologist, 26*(3–4), 325–346. https://doi.org/10.1080/00461520.1991.9653137

Dunn, R., & Honigsfeld, A. (2013). Learning styles: What we know and what we need. *The Educational Forum, 77*(2), 225–232. https://doi.org/10.1080/00131725.2013.765328

Flowerday, T., & Schraw, G. (2003). Effect of choice on cognitive and affective engagement. *The Journal of Educational Research, 96*(4), 207–215. https://doi.org/10.1080/00220670309598810

Keen, D. (2001). *Talent in the new millennium. Research study, 2001–2002, into gifted education in the Bay of Plenty, Otago and Southland regions of New Zealand. Report on year 1 of the program* [Paper presentation]. The Australian Association for Research in Education, Perth, Australia.

Komarraju, M., Karau, S. J., Schmeck, R. R., & Avdic, A. (2011). The Big Five personality traits, learning styles, and academic achievement.

Personality and Individual Differences, 51(4), 472–477. https://doi.org/10.1016/j.paid.2011.04.019

Litman, J., Hutchins, T., & Russon, R. (2005). Epistemic curiosity, feeling-of-knowing, and exploratory behaviour. *Cognition and Emotion, 19*(4), 559–582. https://doi.org/10.1080/02699930441000427

Magner, L. (2000). Reaching all children through differentiated assessment: The 2-5-8 plan. *Gifted Child Today, 23*(3), 48–50. https://doi.org/10.1177/107621750002300313

Patall, E. A. (2013). Constructing motivation through choice, interest, and interestingness. *Journal of Educational Psychology, 105*(2), 522–534. https://doi.org/10.1037/a0030307

Ricca, J. (1984). Learning styles and preferred instructional strategies of gifted students. *Gifted Child Quarterly, 28*(3), 121–126. https://doi.org/10.1177/001698628402800305

Robinson, J., Patall, E. A., & Cooper, H. (2008). The effects of choice on intrinsic motivation and related outcomes: A meta-analysis of research findings. *Psychological Bulletin, 134*(2), 270–300. https://doi.org/10.1037/0033-2909.134.2.270

Sagan, L. L. (2010). Students' choice: Recommendations for environmental and instructional changes in school. *The Clearing House: A Journal of Educational Strategies, Issues and Ideas, 83*(6), 217–222. https://doi.org/10.1080/00098650903505407

Snyder, R. F. (1999). The relationship between learning styles/multiple intelligences and academic achievement of high school students. *The High School Journal, 83*(2), 11–20.

About the Author

After teaching science for more than 15 years, both overseas and in the U.S., **Laurie E. Westphal, Ed.D.,** now works as an independent gifted education and science consultant nationwide. She enjoys developing and presenting staff development on low-stress differentiation strategies and using menus for various districts and conferences, working with teachers to assist them in planning and developing lessons to meet the needs of their advanced students. Laurie currently resides in Houston, TX, and has made it her goal to convert as many teachers as she can to the differentiated lifestyle in the classroom and to share her vision for real-world, product-based lessons that help all students become critical thinkers and effective problem solvers. She is the author of the Differentiating Instruction With Menus series as well as *Hands-On Physical Science* and *Stress-Free Science*.

Common Core State Standards Alignment

This book aligns with an extensive number of the Common Core State Standards for ELA-Literacy. Please visit https://www.prufrock.com/ccss.aspx to download a complete packet of the standards that align with the menus in this book.